Table of Contents

Introduction 6
*The Cypherpunk Movement: Defining Principles and Ideals
.... 6*
The Birth of Cryptocurrencies: Revolutionizing Money and Power 10
The Legacy of Cypherpunks: Privacy, Freedom, and Decentralization 14

Chapter 1: Bitcoin: The First Cryptocurrency 18
Satoshi Nakamoto: The Mysterious Creator of Bitcoin 18
Understanding Bitcoin: The Basics of Blockchain Technology 22
Bitcoin Mining: Securing the Network and Minting New Coins 26
Bitcoin Transactions: Digital Signatures and Peer-to-Peer Transfers 30

Chapter 2: Altcoins and the Expansion of Cryptocurrency 34
The Rise of Altcoins: Diverse Digital Currencies 34
Litecoin: The Silver to Bitcoin's Gold 38
*Ethereum: Smart Contracts and Decentralized Applications
.... 42*
Ripple and Stellar: Facilitating Efficient Cross-Border Payments 47

Chapter 3: Privacy Coins and Anonymity 52
The Need for Privacy: Pseudonymous Transactions.......... 52
Monero: Enhancing Privacy and Fungibility 57
Zcash: Zero-Knowledge Proofs for Selective Transparency
.... 62
Dash: A Focus on User Anonymity and Speed.................... 66

Chapter 4: Blockchain Beyond Currency 71
Blockchain Applications: Beyond Financial Transactions.. 71
Decentralized Finance (DeFi): Smart Contracts in Finance
.... 76
Non-Fungible Tokens (NFTs): Digital Collectibles and
Ownership... 81
Supply Chain Management: Transparency and Traceability
.... 85

Chapter 5: Scalability and Interoperability 90
Scaling Challenges: Addressing the Limitations of
Blockchain... 90
Layer 2 Solutions: Lightning Network and Payment
Channels 95
Interoperability: Bridging Different Blockchains 100
The Future of Scalability: Sharding and Sidechains 105

Chapter 6: Regulation and Challenges 111
Government Responses: Regulations and Legal
Frameworks 111

Copyright © 2023 by Ethan J. Monroe (Author)

All rights reserved. No part of this book may be reproduced or utilized in any form or by any means, electronic or mechanical, including photocopying, recording or by any information storage and retrieval system, without permission in writing from the publisher, except for brief quotations in critical articles or reviews.

The content of this book is based on various sources and is intended for educational and entertainment purposes only. While the author has made every effort to ensure the accuracy, completeness, and reliability of the information provided, the information may be subject to errors, omissions, or inaccuracies. Therefore, the author makes no warranties, express or implied, regarding the content of this book.

Readers are advised to seek the guidance of a licensed professional before attempting any techniques or actions outlined in this book. The author is not responsible for any losses, damages, or injuries that may arise from the use of information contained within. The information provided in this book is not intended to be a substitute for professional advice, and readers should not rely solely on the information presented.

By reading this book, readers acknowledge that the author is not providing legal, financial, medical, or professional advice. Any reliance on the information contained in this book is solely at the reader's own risk.

Thank you for selecting this book as a valuable source of knowledge and inspiration. Our aim is to provide you with insights and information that will enrich your understanding and enhance your personal growth. We appreciate your decision to embark on this journey of discovery with us, and we hope that this book will exceed your expectations and leave a lasting impact on your life.

Title: Cryptonomicon: The Birth of Digital Currency
Subtitle: Tracing the Path from Early Digital Cash Systems to the Revolutionary Emergence of Bitcoin

Series: Cryptonomicon: Unveiling the Roots of Digital Currency
Author: Ethan J. Monroe

Security and Hacks: Protecting Digital Assets *117*
Environmental Impact: Energy Consumption and Sustainability *122*
Social and Economic Implications: Disruption and Adoption *127*

Chapter 7: The Decentralized Future **132**
Decentralized Governance: DAOs and Community Consensus *132*
Web3.0: The Decentralized Internet *138*
The Potential of Cryptocurrencies: Financial Inclusion and Empowerment *143*
Exploring New Frontiers: Quantum Resistance and Post-Blockchain Technologies *148*

Conclusion **153**
The Cypherpunk Ideals in a Cryptocurrency World *153*
Balancing Privacy, Security, and Regulation *157*
Embracing the Decentralized Future *162*

Wordbook **166**
Supplementary Materials **170**

Introduction
The Cypherpunk Movement: Defining Principles and Ideals

In the ever-evolving landscape of technology, there are moments when a group of visionary individuals coalesce around a set of ideals that challenge the established norms and envision a future that empowers individuals and safeguards their digital lives. The Cypherpunk movement, born in the late 1980s and maturing through the 1990s, was one such moment—a crucible of innovation and advocacy that would lay the ideological groundwork for the birth of cryptocurrencies and blockchain technology.

Origins of the Cypherpunk Movement

The seeds of the Cypherpunk movement were sown during an era when the internet was transitioning from an academic network to a global phenomenon. Cypherpunks were individuals who recognized the potential of cryptography to protect personal privacy, secure communication, and foster a society free from undue surveillance. This nascent group shared a common belief: that strong cryptography could be a powerful tool in the hands of ordinary individuals, empowering them to assert their privacy rights in a rapidly digitizing world.

Defining Principles and Ideals

At the heart of the Cypherpunk movement were a set of principles and ideals that formed the philosophical foundation for their actions and endeavors. These principles, often articulated in passionate manifestos and discussions, would come to shape the ethos of the movement and lay the groundwork for the development of decentralized digital currencies and cryptographic protocols.

1. Privacy as a Fundamental Right: The Cypherpunks championed the idea that individuals should have the right to communicate and transact privately. Encryption, they believed, could shield sensitive information from prying eyes and oppressive regimes, fostering a space for free expression and individual autonomy.

2. Decentralization and Empowerment: The concentration of power in centralized institutions, whether governments or corporations, was seen as a threat to personal freedom. The Cypherpunks sought to decentralize control and empower individuals to have greater agency over their digital interactions.

3. Openness and Collaboration: Collaboration was at the core of the Cypherpunk ethos. They believed that cryptographic tools and knowledge should be openly shared, allowing anyone to participate and contribute to the development of secure systems. This collaborative spirit laid

the groundwork for the open-source movement that underpins many cryptocurrency projects today.

4. Technological Innovation: Cypherpunks were technologists at heart. They believed that innovative use of cryptography and technology could lead to solutions that could challenge existing power structures and facilitate a more inclusive digital society.

5. Anonymity and Pseudonymity: In a world where personal identity was increasingly tied to digital footprints, the Cypherpunks advocated for the right to pseudonymity and anonymity. They recognized that privacy didn't just mean shielding information—it also encompassed the ability to transact and interact without revealing one's identity.

The Cypherpunk Manifestos

The movement's ideals were encapsulated in a series of influential manifestos that circulated within the Cypherpunk community and beyond. These manifestos, including the "Crypto Anarchist Manifesto" by Timothy C. May and Eric Hughes, the "A Cypherpunk's Manifesto" by Eric Hughes, and the "Cyphernomicon" by Timothy C. May, articulated the philosophical underpinnings of the movement and highlighted the potential societal impact of cryptographic technology.

Legacy and Impact

The Cypherpunk movement, while relatively niche in its time, laid the groundwork for the profound changes that would come with the advent of cryptocurrencies and blockchain technology. The principles of privacy, decentralization, and empowerment that the Cypherpunks championed would find their realization in the emergence of Bitcoin and subsequent blockchain projects. The movement's legacy can be traced through the narratives of individual Cypherpunks who later became influential figures in the cryptocurrency space.

As we embark on this journey to explore the intricacies of cryptocurrencies and their impact, it's crucial to understand the ideological tapestry woven by the Cypherpunks. Their commitment to privacy, freedom, and decentralization set the stage for the technological revolution we find ourselves amidst today. In the chapters that follow, we will delve into the evolution of cryptocurrencies, the technical innovations that have reshaped finance, and the societal implications that continue to shape our understanding of money, power, and the digital world.

The Birth of Cryptocurrencies: Revolutionizing Money and Power

In the ever-evolving landscape of human civilization, there are rare moments when technological advancements converge with the unquenchable human desire for autonomy and innovation. The emergence of cryptocurrencies represents one such moment—a transformative juncture where technology, economics, and ideology intertwine to challenge conventional notions of money and power.

Unraveling Traditional Finance

The history of money is a tapestry woven with the threads of commerce, trust, and governance. For centuries, currencies were backed by physical assets like gold or silver and were subject to the control of central authorities. The centralized nature of traditional financial systems brought with it a host of challenges, including censorship, inflation, and limited access. Cryptocurrencies emerged as a response to these limitations, driven by the need to rewire the financial landscape and empower individuals with greater control over their wealth.

The Concept of Digital Cash

The groundwork for cryptocurrencies was laid by visionary thinkers like David Chaum, who introduced the concept of digital cash in the 1980s. Chaum's work highlighted the potential of cryptographic techniques to enable secure and private digital transactions. This concept, although revolutionary, faced challenges in implementation due to the lack of a decentralized consensus mechanism that could prevent double-spending without relying on a central authority.

Pre-Bitcoin Attempts: Bit Gold and B-Money

As the digital age advanced, trailblazing cryptographers sought to develop decentralized digital currencies that would address the shortcomings of traditional financial systems. Two notable concepts emerged: Bit Gold proposed by Nick Szabo and B-Money envisioned by Wei Dai. While these ideas laid the groundwork for cryptographic currencies, they faced practical challenges in achieving consensus and scalability without a robust framework like the blockchain.

The Genesis of Bitcoin

The breakthrough that would forever change the course of finance came in 2008, with the publication of the Bitcoin whitepaper by the enigmatic Satoshi Nakamoto. Nakamoto's ingenious combination of existing technologies—cryptography, decentralized consensus, and peer-to-peer networking—culminated in the creation of Bitcoin, the first truly decentralized digital currency.

Bitcoin's whitepaper presented a solution to the double-spending problem through the concept of proof-of-work and introduced the revolutionary idea of the blockchain—a public ledger that would forever change the way transactions were recorded and verified.

Decentralization Redefined

Bitcoin's emergence brought decentralization to the forefront of discussions about money and power. Unlike traditional financial systems, where central banks and governments held sway over monetary policies, Bitcoin's decentralized architecture shifted power to a network of participants who collectively verified transactions and maintained the integrity of the blockchain. This new paradigm had profound implications for trust, security, and the very nature of financial intermediaries.

The Dawn of a New Era

The release of the Bitcoin software in 2009 marked the birth of the world's first cryptocurrency. Its reception was modest at first, confined to a small community of cryptography enthusiasts and early adopters. However, as news of this groundbreaking technology spread, a wave of curiosity and intrigue began to sweep across the digital landscape. The vision of a decentralized, borderless, and censorship-resistant currency captured the imagination of individuals disillusioned with the traditional financial system.

Impact on Money and Power Dynamics

Bitcoin's revolutionary potential was not confined to its technological prowess. It was a challenge to the very fabric of financial power structures that had endured for centuries. Cryptocurrencies posed questions that resonated far beyond code and cryptography. How would governments and central banks respond to a currency they couldn't control or inflate? How would traditional financial intermediaries adapt to a system that rendered their services redundant? These questions sparked debates that rippled through the realms of economics, politics, and philosophy.

Conclusion

As we journey through the pages of this book, we will explore the multifaceted landscape that cryptocurrencies have woven. From their humble beginnings as theoretical concepts to the global phenomenon they are today, cryptocurrencies are a testament to human ingenuity and the power of decentralization. The subsequent chapters will unravel the technical intricacies, societal implications, and the myriad ways in which cryptocurrencies have disrupted established norms, opening doors to new possibilities and challenges that continue to shape our financial future.

The Legacy of Cypherpunks: Privacy, Freedom, and Decentralization

In the annals of technological progress, there are moments when a group of visionary individuals plant the seeds of ideas that germinate, take root, and eventually reshape the very fabric of society. The Cypherpunk movement, often discussed in the context of its technological contributions, left a legacy that extends far beyond lines of code and cryptographic protocols. It bequeathed a legacy that has had a profound impact on the values we associate with privacy, freedom, and the democratization of power.

The Legacy of Privacy

The Cypherpunks championed a revolutionary vision of privacy—one that transcended mere confidentiality and extended into a fundamental right of individuals in the digital realm. The movement's emphasis on strong cryptography was not solely about protecting secrets; it was about empowering individuals to assert control over their personal information. The legacy of the Cypherpunks persists in the modern discourse on privacy, challenging governments, corporations, and society at large to respect the autonomy of digital citizens.

Empowering Individuals

Central to the Cypherpunk ethos was the idea of empowering individuals with the tools to safeguard their own rights and interests. In a world where centralized institutions held the reins of power, the Cypherpunks sought to level the playing field. Their efforts set the stage for a paradigm shift, enabling people to transact, communicate, and engage in a digital realm without surrendering control to intermediaries. This legacy echoes in the rise of cryptocurrencies, where the individual's private key becomes the key to financial autonomy.

Decentralization as a Guiding Principle

Decentralization was more than a technical concept for the Cypherpunks—it was a guiding principle that extended to notions of governance, information dissemination, and beyond. This legacy of decentralization laid the foundation for the blockchain revolution, where networks of participants collaboratively maintain trust without relying on a single authority. As we explore the myriad applications of blockchain beyond cryptocurrencies, we trace the continuation of the Cypherpunk legacy in reshaping industries beyond finance.

Cryptographic Advocacy

The Cypherpunks were not content to merely innovate behind closed doors; they were vocal advocates for their principles. The publication of manifestos and discussions in online forums marked a unique intersection of technology, activism, and philosophy. This legacy of open discourse continues to inspire modern advocates for digital rights, encryption, and the responsible use of technology in preserving individual freedoms.

Challenges to Authority

The Cypherpunks were rebels in their own right—rebels who used cryptography as a weapon to challenge entrenched authorities. Their actions and ideals spurred conversations about the balance of power in a digital age, forcing governments and institutions to confront the evolving landscape of technology and its implications. This legacy of challenging authority remains as a reminder that innovation and advocacy can reshape the course of history.

Societal Impact and Cultural Resonance

The legacy of the Cypherpunks reverberated beyond the confines of their immediate goals. Their influence seeped into popular culture, inspiring narratives of digital vigilantes, hackers, and disruptors who questioned societal norms. This cultural resonance, while often dramatized, highlights the enduring fascination with the idea of individuals wielding technology to enact change and reclaim agency in a digital world.

Conclusion

As we embark on a journey to explore the multifaceted realm of cryptocurrencies and their implications, it's crucial to recognize the guiding hand of the Cypherpunk legacy. The principles of privacy, empowerment, and decentralization that the movement championed continue to shape our understanding of digital interactions, individual rights, and the role of technology in shaping our world. In the subsequent chapters, we will delve into the technical intricacies, real-world applications, and ethical considerations that have unfolded as a result of this legacy, shedding light on the intricate tapestry that binds the past, present, and future of the digital age.

Chapter 1: Bitcoin: The First Cryptocurrency
Satoshi Nakamoto: The Mysterious Creator of Bitcoin

In the realm of technological history, there are few enigmatic figures as captivating as Satoshi Nakamoto, the pseudonymous creator of Bitcoin. Nakamoto's identity remains shrouded in mystery, adding an aura of intrigue to the revolutionary invention that shook the foundations of finance and technology. As we delve into the origins of Bitcoin, understanding the enigma behind its creator becomes an essential part of unraveling the narrative.

The Genesis of an Idea

Bitcoin didn't materialize out of thin air—it was the culmination of a confluence of ideas, technologies, and a deep-rooted desire for change. Nakamoto's journey towards the creation of Bitcoin can be traced back to discussions in online cryptography forums, where the concept of decentralized digital currencies was beginning to take shape. The philosophical ideals of the Cypherpunk movement laid the groundwork for Nakamoto's innovative vision.

The Pseudonym: Satoshi Nakamoto

The name "Satoshi Nakamoto" first appeared in the whitepaper titled "Bitcoin: A Peer-to-Peer Electronic Cash System," published in October 2008. Whether a single individual or a group, Nakamoto chose to remain hidden behind a pseudonym. This deliberate anonymity created an environment where the technology itself took center stage, free from the distractions of personal identity or celebrity.

The Whitepaper: A Blueprint for Disruption

Nakamoto's whitepaper, released at the peak of the global financial crisis, presented a revolutionary solution to many of the problems plaguing traditional financial systems. The whitepaper introduced a system that eliminated the need for intermediaries, allowed for secure peer-to-peer transactions, and ensured a decentralized consensus mechanism. The concept of proof-of-work was key to preventing double-spending and providing security.

The Launch of Bitcoin

On January 3, 2009, Nakamoto mined the first block of the Bitcoin blockchain, known as the "genesis block." This block contained a message referencing a headline from that day's newspaper, underlining Nakamoto's intention to establish a timestamp for the inception of Bitcoin. The creation of the genesis block marked the birth of the world's first cryptocurrency.

Early Collaborators and Communications

Nakamoto's creation didn't emerge in isolation. Discussions in online forums and early interactions with developers, including Hal Finney, revealed Nakamoto's dedication to refining the concept and codebase. Nakamoto's communications were typically brief and focused on technical aspects, avoiding personal or ideological discussions. The language used in these communications continues to be analyzed in attempts to uncover Nakamoto's true identity or origin.

Disappearance and Legacy

In 2010, Nakamoto handed over the reins of the Bitcoin project to other developers and gradually faded from the public eye. Nakamoto's exit was as enigmatic as the initial entrance, leaving behind a creation that had ignited a technological revolution. While the figure of Nakamoto retreated from the limelight, the legacy of the creation persisted and grew.

Speculations and Theories

Over the years, numerous theories and individuals have been proposed as the potential true identity of Satoshi Nakamoto. From computer scientists to economists, the search for Nakamoto's identity has become a captivating puzzle, captivating both the cryptocurrency community and the wider public. Yet, whether the identity is revealed or not, Nakamoto's lasting contribution is undeniable.

Impact and Imagination

The mystique surrounding Nakamoto's identity adds an air of mythology to the origins of Bitcoin. The deliberate decision to remain anonymous allowed the technology to be embraced for its own merits, rather than relying on the personality cult often associated with inventors. Nakamoto's approach revolutionized how we perceive innovation and created a template for future projects to embrace decentralized and open development.

Conclusion

Satoshi Nakamoto, the enigmatic creator of Bitcoin, remains a beacon of inspiration for the cryptocurrency community and beyond. The decision to remain anonymous, combined with the brilliance of the ideas presented in the Bitcoin whitepaper, set in motion a transformation that continues to reverberate across the world. The subsequent chapters will delve deeper into the foundational concepts introduced by Nakamoto, the evolution of Bitcoin, and the far-reaching implications of this revolutionary creation.

Understanding Bitcoin: The Basics of Blockchain Technology

In the world of digital innovation, few concepts have captured the collective imagination as profoundly as Bitcoin and its underlying technology, the blockchain. As we journey through the intricacies of the first cryptocurrency, it's essential to grasp the fundamental principles of the blockchain—a groundbreaking invention that transcends Bitcoin itself and serves as the backbone of countless decentralized systems.

The Birth of the Blockchain

The blockchain, often referred to as a distributed ledger, emerged as a solution to the double-spending problem that had plagued previous attempts at digital currency. Satoshi Nakamoto's whitepaper introduced the idea of a decentralized and transparent ledger that would record all transactions without the need for a central authority. This novel solution opened the door to the creation of trustless networks and laid the foundation for Bitcoin's groundbreaking architecture.

Decentralization and Consensus

At the heart of the blockchain lies the concept of decentralization. Unlike traditional databases that rely on a single central authority, the blockchain is maintained by a network of participants spread across the globe. This decentralized structure eliminates single points of failure, making the system robust, resistant to censorship, and less susceptible to attacks. Consensus mechanisms, such as proof-of-work, ensure that all participants agree on the state of the ledger.

The Blocks: Building the Chain

The blockchain is aptly named—the chain is composed of individual blocks, each containing a list of transactions. Each block is linked to the previous one, creating an immutable and chronological sequence of transactions. This structure ensures that once a block is added to the chain, it cannot be altered without invalidating all subsequent blocks. This immutability guarantees the integrity of the transaction history.

Decentralized Trust

The blockchain's decentralized nature redefines trust in the digital realm. In traditional systems, trust is often placed in intermediaries or central authorities. With the blockchain, trust is distributed across the network. Transactions are verified by a consensus mechanism, and the result is a tamper-resistant record that can be audited by anyone. This innovation not only reduces the need for intermediaries but also shifts the power dynamic between institutions and individuals.

Public vs. Private Blockchains

While Bitcoin's blockchain is public and open to anyone, the concept of blockchain has also been embraced by private enterprises seeking to harness its benefits for internal processes. Private blockchains restrict access to authorized participants, balancing the benefits of decentralization with the need for privacy and control. However, the distinction between public and private blockchains raises questions about the essence of decentralization and the balance between openness and confidentiality.

Smart Contracts: The Next Evolution

Beyond serving as a ledger for financial transactions, the blockchain paved the way for smart contracts—an innovation that extends the concept of trustless interactions to a wide range of applications. Smart contracts are self-executing programs that automatically execute predefined actions when certain conditions are met. These contracts eliminate the need for intermediaries, streamline processes, and have the potential to revolutionize industries such as law, real estate, and supply chain management.

Scalability Challenges

While the blockchain offers a transformative solution to many problems, it also faces scalability challenges. The decentralized nature of the blockchain means that each transaction must be verified by a network of participants, leading to potential bottlenecks. Various solutions, such as off-chain transactions and layer 2 solutions like the Lightning Network, have been proposed to address scalability concerns.

Conclusion

As we delve into the intricacies of Bitcoin and its foundational technology—the blockchain—it becomes clear that this invention transcends the realm of finance. The blockchain's innovative architecture, rooted in decentralization and cryptographic principles, has ignited a paradigm shift in how we conceive of trust, transparency, and digital interactions. The chapters ahead will continue to explore the nuances of this technology, its applications beyond currencies, and its potential to reshape industries, governance, and the fabric of our digital society.

Bitcoin Mining: Securing the Network and Minting New Coins

As we continue our exploration of Bitcoin—the pioneer of cryptocurrencies—it's essential to delve into the mechanics that enable its functionality. At the heart of Bitcoin's operations lies a revolutionary process known as mining. This process not only secures the network's integrity but also serves as the mechanism for creating new coins, establishing the foundation upon which the entire ecosystem rests.

The Genesis of Mining

Bitcoin's creation presented a groundbreaking solution to the double-spending problem through the decentralized and transparent ledger of the blockchain. However, the challenge of maintaining the integrity of this ledger required a novel consensus mechanism. Enter mining—a process that harnesses computational power to verify transactions and secure the network.

Proof-of-Work: The Mining Mechanism

Bitcoin's consensus mechanism, known as proof-of-work (PoW), is the cornerstone of its security model. PoW requires miners to solve complex mathematical puzzles, effectively competing against each other to be the first to find a solution. The solution, also known as a "hash," is then added to the block, and the block is added to the blockchain. This process not only verifies transactions but also establishes the chronological order of events.

Mining Rewards: Incentives for Participation

Mining is not a philanthropic endeavor; it's driven by a carefully designed incentive structure. Miners who successfully add a new block to the blockchain are rewarded with newly minted Bitcoins and transaction fees. This system serves a dual purpose: it introduces new coins into circulation while ensuring that miners have a vested interest in the network's security and functionality.

The Halving: Scarcity and Reward Reduction

One of the most intriguing aspects of Bitcoin's mining process is the halving event. Approximately every four years, the number of new Bitcoins issued as rewards for mining is halved. This event is programmed into the Bitcoin protocol and serves to mimic the scarcity of precious metals like gold. The halving has a profound impact on the supply of new coins and adds an element of scarcity to Bitcoin's monetary policy.

Mining Pools: Collaborative Power

As Bitcoin's popularity grew, individual miners faced an increasing challenge in competing against larger mining operations with significant computational power. This led to the rise of mining pools—groups of miners who combine their computational resources to collectively solve the mathematical puzzles. While this approach ensures more consistent rewards, it also raises questions about centralization and potential vulnerabilities.

Energy Consumption and Environmental Concerns

The PoW mechanism, while effective, demands substantial computational power, leading to energy consumption that has sparked debates about Bitcoin's environmental impact. Critics argue that the energy footprint associated with mining is unsustainable and incompatible with global efforts to combat climate change. Proponents, on the other hand, contend that Bitcoin's incentivized security model justifies the energy expenditure.

Evolution and Adaptation

Bitcoin's mining landscape has evolved since its inception. What started as a hobbyist endeavor has transformed into a competitive and professional industry with specialized hardware and data centers. Miners constantly seek more efficient hardware and strategies to optimize energy consumption and increase their chances of solving the cryptographic puzzles.

Mining Beyond Coins: Proof-of-Work Variants

While Bitcoin's PoW remains the most well-known form of mining, the concept has been adapted for other purposes beyond securing a cryptocurrency network. Projects like Ethereum, among others, have introduced variations of PoW to enable more than just transaction validation, including the execution of smart contracts and decentralized applications.

Conclusion

Bitcoin mining stands as a testament to the ingenious fusion of technology, economics, and incentives. It's a process that not only secures the network but also underpins the creation of new coins. As we traverse the complexities of the Bitcoin ecosystem, understanding mining unveils the intricate dance between computation and consensus, security and scarcity. The subsequent chapters will continue to unveil the layers of Bitcoin's foundation, exploring its various applications and the ways in which it has transformed the world of finance, technology, and beyond.

Bitcoin Transactions: Digital Signatures and Peer-to-Peer Transfers

In our exploration of Bitcoin's foundational components, we encounter the heart of its functionality—transactions. These digital exchanges of value form the backbone of the cryptocurrency's utility, enabling individuals to transfer assets across borders and without intermediaries. Understanding how Bitcoin transactions work, from digital signatures to peer-to-peer transfers, sheds light on the innovation that has revolutionized the concept of ownership and exchange.

Digital Signatures: Unveiling Ownership

Bitcoin transactions begin with digital signatures, cryptographic mechanisms that serve as proof of ownership and authenticity. When a user wishes to send Bitcoin to another address, they create a digital signature using their private key. This signature is then appended to the transaction data, effectively proving that the sender possesses the corresponding private key. This cryptographic proof ensures that only the rightful owner can initiate transactions.

Public and Private Keys: The Key Pair

The foundation of digital signatures lies in the concept of public and private key pairs. The public key serves as an address through which funds can be received, while the private key is a secret known only to the owner. The public key is derived from the private key, and the cryptographic relationship between the two ensures that data signed with the private key can be verified using the corresponding public key.

The Transaction Structure: Inputs and Outputs

Bitcoin transactions involve inputs and outputs. Inputs refer to the sources of funds that are being spent in the transaction, and outputs designate the addresses to which the funds are being sent. To spend Bitcoin, a user must reference unspent transaction outputs (UTXOs) as inputs in their transaction. The outputs designate the new owner(s) of the Bitcoin being transferred.

Transaction Validation: The Role of Miners

Once a transaction is created, it must be verified and added to the blockchain. Miners play a pivotal role in this process. Before being included in a block, a transaction must be confirmed by miners, who verify its validity by checking the digital signatures, the sufficiency of funds, and other rules. Once verified, the transaction is added to a candidate block, and the miner competes to solve the proof-of-work puzzle to add the block to the blockchain.

Peer-to-Peer Transfers: Disintermediating Trust

One of Bitcoin's groundbreaking achievements is its ability to enable peer-to-peer transactions without intermediaries. Traditionally, transactions required trusted intermediaries such as banks or payment processors to ensure that funds were transferred securely. With Bitcoin, the blockchain's transparent ledger and cryptographic mechanisms eliminate the need for these intermediaries, allowing individuals to transact directly.

Transaction Fees: Incentivizing Miners

While miners are rewarded with newly minted Bitcoins for their efforts, transactions often include additional incentives known as transaction fees. These fees are paid by the sender as compensation for including their transaction in the blockchain. During times of network congestion, users may offer higher fees to expedite the confirmation of their transactions.

Security and Anonymity

Bitcoin's transparency is both a strength and a potential concern. While all transactions are recorded on the public blockchain, the identities of the participants remain pseudonymous. This aspect has sparked discussions about the balance between privacy and transparency. Techniques such as coin mixing and using multiple addresses can enhance privacy by obfuscating the origin of funds.

Future Possibilities: Beyond Transactions

As the Bitcoin network continues to evolve, advancements are being explored to enhance the efficiency and capabilities of transactions. Technologies like the Lightning Network aim to enable faster and cheaper microtransactions by conducting certain transactions off-chain, while retaining the security of the main blockchain.

Conclusion

Bitcoin transactions represent more than the movement of coins—they embody a transformation in the way value is exchanged, ownership is proven, and trust is established. The blend of cryptography, peer-to-peer networking, and decentralized consensus forms the basis of a revolutionary financial system that transcends geographical boundaries and challenges traditional intermediaries. As we progress through the subsequent chapters, we will further unravel the multifaceted facets of Bitcoin's impact on finance, technology, and society.

Chapter 2: Altcoins and the Expansion of Cryptocurrency

The Rise of Altcoins: Diverse Digital Currencies

As the concept of cryptocurrency gained traction in the wake of Bitcoin's emergence, a new wave of innovation began to take shape. Altcoins—alternative cryptocurrencies—emerged as experiments and alternatives to Bitcoin, each introducing unique features, governance models, and use cases. In this chapter, we delve into the diverse landscape of altcoins, exploring the motivations behind their creation and the impact they've had on the broader cryptocurrency ecosystem.

Altcoins: A Natural Progression

The success of Bitcoin as the first cryptocurrency laid the groundwork for the emergence of altcoins. While Bitcoin demonstrated the potential of decentralized digital currencies, its limitations—such as scalability issues and proof-of-work energy consumption—inspired developers to explore alternative solutions. Altcoins aimed to address these limitations, offering new features and technological advancements.

Motivations for Altcoin Creation

Altcoins were born out of various motivations. Some aimed to improve upon Bitcoin's shortcomings, introducing innovations like faster transaction confirmations, improved scalability, and more energy-efficient consensus mechanisms. Others sought to experiment with new use cases, such as enabling privacy-focused transactions, incorporating smart contract functionality, or catering to specific industries.

Litecoin: The Silver to Bitcoin's Gold

One of the earliest and most influential altcoins is Litecoin. Created by Charlie Lee in 2011, Litecoin aimed to be a "lighter" version of Bitcoin, with faster block confirmation times and a different hashing algorithm. Litecoin's launch introduced the concept of script mining and introduced a new community of developers and enthusiasts.

Variety of Consensus Mechanisms

Altcoins have experimented with various consensus mechanisms beyond proof-of-work. Some have embraced proof-of-stake, which replaces energy-intensive mining with the concept of "staking" coins to secure the network. Others have explored delegated proof-of-stake, proof-of-authority, and other hybrid mechanisms, each offering distinct trade-offs in terms of security, decentralization, and scalability.

Privacy Coins: Enhanced Anonymity

Privacy coins emerged as a response to concerns about the privacy and fungibility of cryptocurrencies. Coins like Monero, Zcash, and Dash integrated advanced cryptographic techniques to offer enhanced anonymity and improved privacy features. These coins aim to provide users with the ability to transact confidentially and shield their financial activities from prying eyes.

Smart Contracts and Decentralized Applications

Ethereum, launched in 2015, pioneered the concept of smart contracts—self-executing programs that automatically execute predefined actions when specific conditions are met. Ethereum's blockchain not only facilitates peer-to-peer transactions but also serves as a platform for decentralized applications (dApps) that can range from decentralized finance (DeFi) protocols to digital collectibles.

Ripple and Stellar: Efficient Cross-Border Payments

While many altcoins sought to compete with Bitcoin by offering similar features, others aimed to tackle specific niches within the financial industry. Ripple and Stellar, for instance, focus on enabling efficient cross-border payments and remittances. These coins emphasize speed, cost-effectiveness, and interoperability with traditional financial systems.

Challenges and Concerns

The proliferation of altcoins has not been without challenges. The sheer number of projects vying for attention and adoption has led to concerns about oversaturation, scams, and lack of real-world utility. Additionally, the rise of altcoins has raised questions about the fragmentation of the cryptocurrency ecosystem and the potential dilution of resources and focus.

The Role of Altcoins in Innovation

While not all altcoins have achieved long-lasting success, their presence in the cryptocurrency landscape has contributed to ongoing innovation. The competition and experimentation spurred by altcoins have led to the exploration of diverse technologies, the refinement of consensus mechanisms, and the introduction of novel use cases.

Conclusion

The rise of altcoins marked a critical turning point in the evolution of the cryptocurrency ecosystem. These diverse digital currencies demonstrated the adaptability and flexibility of blockchain technology, while also highlighting the challenges inherent in launching and maintaining successful projects. As we venture further into the world of altcoins and their impact on the broader financial landscape, we will uncover the various ways they have expanded the realm of possibility for blockchain applications and reshaped the dynamics of decentralized innovation.

Litecoin: The Silver to Bitcoin's Gold

As the cryptocurrency landscape continued to evolve after Bitcoin's emergence, a new contender entered the scene—one that aimed to complement and enhance the capabilities of the pioneer cryptocurrency. Litecoin, often referred to as the "silver to Bitcoin's gold," captured the attention of the community with its unique approach, faster transaction confirmation times, and commitment to innovation. In this section, we delve into the story of Litecoin's creation, its key features, and the lasting impact it has had on the broader cryptocurrency ecosystem.

The Genesis of Litecoin

Litecoin was conceived by Charlie Lee, a former Google engineer, and was launched in October 2011. Lee's motivation for creating Litecoin was to address some of the limitations of Bitcoin while staying true to the core principles of decentralization and open source development. Litecoin sought to offer a cryptocurrency that could complement Bitcoin's store of value narrative by emphasizing its utility as a medium of exchange.

Faster Block Confirmation Times

One of Litecoin's most notable features is its faster block confirmation times. While Bitcoin aims for an average block time of 10 minutes, Litecoin boasts a block time of just

2.5 minutes. This faster confirmation time was designed to enhance the speed of transactions, making Litecoin more suitable for day-to-day use and microtransactions. The shorter block time also contributes to Litecoin's potential scalability advantages.

Scrypt Mining: A Different Approach

Litecoin introduced a novel consensus mechanism known as scrypt mining. Unlike Bitcoin's proof-of-work mechanism, which relies on the SHA-256 hashing algorithm, Litecoin's scrypt algorithm aimed to democratize the mining process. Scrypt was chosen to be memory-intensive, making it resistant to the ASIC (Application-Specific Integrated Circuit) mining hardware that had started to dominate Bitcoin mining.

Community and Development

Litecoin quickly garnered a dedicated community of enthusiasts and developers. Its active GitHub repository and frequent updates demonstrated the team's commitment to continuous improvement. The open and collaborative nature of Litecoin's development process mirrored the ethos of the broader cryptocurrency community and contributed to the project's ongoing relevance.

Litecoin's Role in the Ecosystem

While Bitcoin remained the flagship cryptocurrency, Litecoin found its place as a complementary asset within the broader cryptocurrency ecosystem. Its faster confirmation times and scrypt mining mechanism made it a viable option for daily transactions, micropayments, and small-scale remittances. This niche positioning earned Litecoin its moniker as "digital silver," offering a more accessible entry point for those interested in cryptocurrency.

Litecoin's Influence on the Market

Litecoin's creation sparked a wave of innovation in the altcoin space. Its introduction of scrypt mining inspired the development of other altcoins with unique consensus mechanisms and features. Litecoin's focus on usability and transaction speed also set a precedent for subsequent altcoins to prioritize practical utility in addition to store of value.

Challenges and Adaptations

Like any evolving project, Litecoin faced its share of challenges and adaptations. While it established itself as one of the leading altcoins, it also encountered competition from other projects seeking to address similar goals. Moreover, the changing landscape of technology and market dynamics required Litecoin to adapt to shifting demands and preferences.

Continued Evolution and Innovation

Litecoin has continued to evolve over the years, introducing enhancements such as the Lightning Network, atomic swaps, and partnerships aimed at expanding its use cases. Its ongoing commitment to technical innovation and community-driven development has allowed it to maintain its relevance and continue contributing to the broader cryptocurrency narrative.

Conclusion

Litecoin's journey as the "silver to Bitcoin's gold" exemplifies the spirit of exploration and innovation that defined the early years of the cryptocurrency ecosystem. Its unique features, commitment to usability, and role as a complementary asset have contributed to its enduring presence in the market. As we delve further into the landscape of altcoins, Litecoin's legacy reminds us of the diverse avenues for exploration and experimentation that cryptocurrencies continue to offer.

Ethereum: Smart Contracts and Decentralized Applications

In the evolving tapestry of cryptocurrencies and blockchain technology, Ethereum stands as a monumental shift—a platform that extends beyond simple transactions to enable a new era of decentralized applications (dApps) and programmable contracts. Ethereum's innovation lies not just in its native cryptocurrency, Ether (ETH), but in its ability to execute complex code on its blockchain, revolutionizing industries and introducing the concept of smart contracts. In this section, we delve into the genesis of Ethereum, its unique features, and the transformative impact it has had on the realm of decentralized applications.

The Birth of Ethereum

Vitalik Buterin, a young programmer and cryptocurrency enthusiast, conceptualized Ethereum in late 2013. Buterin's vision was to create a blockchain platform that could execute arbitrary code and enable the development of decentralized applications beyond simple transactions. Ethereum's initial whitepaper, published in 2013, laid out the technical specifications and principles behind the platform's creation.

The Ethereum Virtual Machine (EVM)

At the core of Ethereum's innovation is the Ethereum Virtual Machine (EVM), a Turing-complete virtual machine that enables the execution of smart contracts. The EVM processes code in a decentralized manner, ensuring that computations are verifiable and consistent across the network. This unique capability unlocked a world of possibilities beyond simple cryptocurrency transfers.

Smart Contracts: Code as Law

Smart contracts are self-executing programs that automatically execute predefined actions when specific conditions are met. These contracts operate without the need for intermediaries, guaranteeing trust and transparency. By translating contractual agreements into code, Ethereum introduced a new paradigm where code becomes law, removing the need for traditional legal intermediaries.

Decentralized Applications (dApps)

Ethereum's introduction of smart contracts paved the way for the development of decentralized applications, or dApps. These applications leverage the blockchain's decentralized nature and smart contract functionality to offer new and innovative services across various industries. From decentralized finance (DeFi) protocols to supply chain management systems, the range of dApps has grown exponentially, reshaping the way we interact with digital services.

The ICO Boom and Tokenization

Ethereum's flexibility also enabled the proliferation of Initial Coin Offerings (ICOs)—a fundraising method that allowed projects to create and distribute their own tokens on the Ethereum blockchain. The ICO boom of 2017 showcased the platform's potential for tokenization, transforming how startups and projects raised capital. While ICOs had a transformative impact, they also raised regulatory concerns and highlighted the need for responsible token issuance.

Challenges and Scalability

Ethereum's success brought with it new challenges, most notably scalability. As the demand for dApps and transactions grew, Ethereum's network faced congestion, higher fees, and slower confirmation times. This led to the exploration of various scaling solutions, including sharding, layer 2 solutions, and the transition to Ethereum 2.0—an upgrade aimed at improving scalability, security, and energy efficiency.

The Road to Ethereum 2.0

Ethereum 2.0, also known as Eth2 or Serenity, represents a multi-phase upgrade that will transition Ethereum from a proof-of-work (PoW) to a proof-of-stake

(PoS) consensus mechanism. This shift aims to improve scalability, reduce energy consumption, and increase network security. The upgrade includes the introduction of the Beacon Chain, shard chains, and other improvements that lay the groundwork for Ethereum's next phase.

Ethereum's Cultural Impact

Beyond its technological advancements, Ethereum has fostered a community of developers, entrepreneurs, and enthusiasts who share a vision of decentralized innovation. The platform's open-source nature, hackathons, and developer grants have nurtured a culture of collaboration and experimentation, inspiring the creation of new protocols, tools, and applications that extend the boundaries of what is possible.

Conclusion

Ethereum's emergence marked a pivotal moment in the evolution of blockchain technology. Its introduction of smart contracts and decentralized applications expanded the use cases beyond simple transactions, transforming industries and enabling the creation of entirely new digital ecosystems. As we continue our exploration of altcoins and their impact, Ethereum serves as a beacon of decentralized innovation, exemplifying the potential of blockchain to reshape the way we interact with technology, finance, and the world around us.

Ripple and Stellar: Facilitating Efficient Cross-Border Payments

As the cryptocurrency landscape expanded, new altcoins emerged with specific goals in mind, aiming to address real-world challenges in innovative ways. Ripple and Stellar, two prominent altcoins, set their sights on revolutionizing the traditional cross-border payments industry. In this section, we delve into the stories of Ripple and Stellar, exploring their unique approaches, partnerships, and the impact they've had on reshaping global remittances and financial transactions.

Ripple: Transforming Cross-Border Transactions

Ripple, founded in 2012 by Chris Larsen and Jed McCaleb, embarked on a mission to tackle the inefficiencies and complexities of cross-border payments. At its core, Ripple introduced a unique consensus algorithm known as the Ripple Protocol Consensus Algorithm (RPCA). Unlike traditional proof-of-work or proof-of-stake mechanisms, RPCA leveraged a consensus process that focused on validating transactions through a network of trusted nodes, making it more energy-efficient and suited for financial institutions.

The XRP Ledger and XRP Token

Central to Ripple's ecosystem is the XRP Ledger, a blockchain designed to facilitate fast and low-cost cross-border transactions. XRP, the native token of the Ripple network, serves as a bridge currency that enables seamless and instant transfers of value between different fiat currencies. The XRP Ledger's design and consensus algorithm make it capable of processing thousands of transactions per second, positioning it as a potential solution for real-time settlements.

Partnerships and Adoption

Ripple's strategy involved building partnerships with financial institutions and payment service providers. Its flagship product, RippleNet, offered a network for global payments and remittances, leveraging XRP for liquidity management. Ripple's partnerships with established players in the financial sector allowed it to integrate its technology into existing systems, potentially streamlining cross-border payments for individuals and businesses.

Stellar: Inclusive Financial Infrastructure

Stellar, co-founded by Jed McCaleb after his involvement with Ripple, aimed to create an open and inclusive financial infrastructure that provided access to the global economy for everyone. Stellar's consensus protocol, the Stellar Consensus Protocol (SCP), relied on a federated model in which a select group of validators agreed on the state of the network. This approach aimed to strike a balance between decentralization and efficiency.

The Lumens (XLM) Token

Stellar introduced the Lumens (XLM) token as the native asset of the network. XLM serves multiple purposes, including facilitating cross-border payments and acting as a bridge currency between different fiat currencies. Stellar's vision extended beyond just payments, focusing on financial inclusion and providing access to services such as micropayments and remittances for underserved populations.

Stellar's Focus on Tokenization

Stellar's protocol was designed with tokenization in mind, allowing users to create and issue custom tokens representing various assets. This approach opened the door for creating digital representations of traditional assets, such as fiat currencies, commodities, and real estate. Stellar's focus on tokenization aimed to facilitate the seamless exchange of value and assets within its ecosystem.

Financial Inclusion and Use Cases

Both Ripple and Stellar shared a common focus on addressing the challenges of cross-border payments, but Stellar's emphasis on financial inclusion set it apart. Stellar aimed to enable individuals in underserved regions to access financial services and participate in the global economy. The platform's use cases ranged from remittances to microfinance, highlighting its potential to empower individuals who lack traditional banking services.

Interoperability and Collaborations

Stellar's approach to interoperability extended beyond its platform. The Stellar Development Foundation partnered with various organizations and institutions to promote cross-border collaboration and facilitate the flow of information and value. Stellar's open-source nature and commitment to interoperability positioned it as a potential bridge between different financial systems and networks.

Challenges and Future Prospects

While both Ripple and Stellar demonstrated potential in transforming cross-border payments, they faced challenges, including regulatory scrutiny and questions about centralization. Ripple's legal battles with regulatory authorities raised questions about the status of XRP as a security. Stellar navigated similar challenges while striving to achieve its mission of financial inclusion.

Conclusion

Ripple and Stellar, with their distinct approaches and goals, have contributed to reshaping the landscape of cross-border payments. Their innovations reflect the broader shift toward leveraging blockchain technology to address inefficiencies and create more accessible financial systems. As we explore the world of altcoins and their influence, Ripple and Stellar exemplify the power of cryptocurrency to transcend borders and redefine the way value is transferred on a global scale.

Chapter 3: Privacy Coins and Anonymity

The Need for Privacy: Pseudonymous Transactions

In the world of cryptocurrencies, privacy has emerged as a critical concern for individuals seeking to maintain their financial autonomy and protect sensitive information. Privacy coins, a category of cryptocurrencies specifically designed to enhance user privacy, have gained prominence by addressing these concerns. This chapter delves into the motivations behind the need for privacy in transactions, the concept of pseudonymous transactions, and how privacy coins have evolved to provide enhanced privacy features for users.

The Importance of Privacy in a Transparent World

As cryptocurrencies gained mainstream attention, the transparency of blockchain technology posed challenges for users who desired financial privacy. In traditional financial systems, transactions are often private by default, with individuals' financial activities shielded from public scrutiny. However, the transparent nature of most cryptocurrencies allowed anyone to view transaction details, potentially compromising user privacy.

Pseudonymity: Balancing Anonymity and Transparency

Cryptocurrencies introduced the concept of pseudonymity—a middle ground between complete anonymity and complete transparency. Pseudonymous transactions involve the use of cryptographic addresses rather than real-world identities. While transactions are publicly recorded on the blockchain, the link between an address and a real identity is obfuscated. This approach maintains a level of transparency while offering a degree of privacy.

Risks of Transparent Transactions

Transparent transactions can lead to various risks, including the potential for third parties to track users' spending habits, analyze transaction history, and potentially de-anonymize users. This poses security concerns, particularly when transactions involve large sums or sensitive personal information. Privacy coins emerged as a response to these risks, aiming to provide enhanced privacy features without compromising the benefits of cryptocurrencies.

Privacy Coins: Enhancing Transaction Privacy

Privacy coins, such as Monero, Zcash, and Dash, introduced advanced cryptographic techniques to enhance transaction privacy. These coins aimed to provide users with the ability to transact confidentially and shield their financial activities from prying eyes. The methods employed by privacy coins vary, but they generally revolve around obfuscating transaction details and enhancing the fungibility of coins.

Monero: Ring Signatures and Stealth Addresses

Monero, one of the pioneering privacy coins, introduced technologies like ring signatures and stealth addresses. Ring signatures allow transactions to be signed with multiple keys, making it difficult to determine the actual sender. Stealth addresses generate unique one-time addresses for each transaction, further obscuring the link between sender and receiver.

Zcash: Zero-Knowledge Proofs for Selective Transparency

Zcash introduced zero-knowledge proofs, a cryptographic technique that enables a verifier to confirm the validity of a statement without revealing any specific information. Zcash transactions can be either transparent or shielded, offering users the choice between selective transparency and complete privacy.

Dash: PrivateSend Mixing and Speed

Dash, while offering optional privacy features, introduced PrivateSend—a mixing mechanism that blends multiple transactions to obscure the source and destination of funds. Dash also prioritizes speed and ease of use alongside privacy, aiming to provide a seamless experience for users who desire enhanced privacy without sacrificing transaction efficiency.

Privacy and Regulatory Concerns

The rise of privacy coins has led to discussions about the balance between privacy and regulatory compliance. While privacy coins offer valuable tools for preserving individual autonomy, concerns have been raised about their potential misuse for illicit activities. Regulatory challenges have led to varying approaches by different jurisdictions, with some exchanges delisting privacy coins to comply with regulatory requirements.

The Broader Implications

Beyond individual privacy, privacy coins have broader implications for the cryptocurrency ecosystem. They highlight the importance of user choice and the need for innovative solutions to protect privacy in a digital age. Privacy coins also underscore the evolution of cryptocurrencies beyond basic financial transactions, opening doors to new applications and use cases.

Conclusion

The need for privacy in the realm of cryptocurrencies is undeniable, as users seek to preserve their financial autonomy and protect sensitive information. Pseudonymous transactions offer a balance between transparency and privacy, and privacy coins have emerged as a response to this demand. Their innovative approaches to transaction privacy, from ring signatures to zero-knowledge proofs, have sparked discussions about privacy's role in the digital age and its potential to reshape the landscape of financial transactions. As we delve deeper into the world of privacy coins and their impact, we'll explore the technologies and strategies that empower users to transact securely in an interconnected world.

Monero: Enhancing Privacy and Fungibility

In the realm of privacy coins, Monero stands as a pioneering force, embodying the ideals of transactional privacy and fungibility. Designed to address the limitations of transparent cryptocurrencies, Monero introduces a unique set of privacy features that obscure transaction details and enhance user anonymity. This section delves into the story of Monero's creation, the innovative technologies that underpin its privacy features, and its impact on reshaping the narrative around financial privacy and fungibility.

The Genesis of Monero

Monero, launched in April 2014, emerged as a response to the privacy concerns inherent in transparent cryptocurrencies like Bitcoin. Conceived by a group of pseudonymous developers under the alias "thankful_for_today," Monero aimed to offer enhanced privacy and fungibility without compromising decentralization and security. Its name, derived from the Esperanto word for "coin," reflected its commitment to preserving financial privacy in a world of increasing transparency.

Ring Signatures: Obfuscating Transaction Origin

At the core of Monero's privacy features lies the concept of ring signatures. Traditional cryptographic signatures confirm the authenticity of a transaction by proving that the sender possesses the private key associated with the public address. Ring signatures take this concept further by creating a group of potential signers, or "ring," among which the actual signer is indistinguishable. This confounds efforts to trace the transaction back to its origin.

Stealth Addresses: Obscuring Receivers

Monero's privacy toolbox also includes stealth addresses. When a user initiates a transaction, Monero generates a one-time destination address for the receiver, known as a stealth address. This means that even though the transaction is recorded on the blockchain, the recipient's identity remains hidden, offering a significant improvement in privacy compared to traditional transparent blockchains.

Confidential Transactions: Concealing Amounts

Confidential Transactions further enhance Monero's privacy by obscuring transaction amounts. In Bitcoin, transaction amounts are visible on the blockchain, potentially enabling third parties to deduce financial habits. Monero's Confidential Transactions use cryptographic methods to hide transaction amounts while ensuring that the transaction remains valid and secure.

RingCT: Privacy for Amounts and Destinations

Building upon Confidential Transactions, Monero introduced Ring Confidential Transactions (RingCT). This technology extends the concept of ring signatures to cover transaction amounts as well as sender and receiver addresses. RingCT enables both the origin and destination of a transaction to be obfuscated, providing a high level of privacy across all transaction components.

Enhancing Fungibility

Monero's focus on privacy directly impacts its fungibility—the property of each unit of a currency being interchangeable with any other unit. Fungibility is essential for a functional currency, as it ensures that all units are treated equally, regardless of their transaction history. Monero's privacy features enhance fungibility by making it nearly impossible to trace transaction history and distinguish between coins.

Obstacles and Challenges

While Monero's privacy features provide valuable benefits, they have also attracted attention from regulators and law enforcement agencies concerned about potential misuse for illicit activities. Some exchanges have faced delisting pressure due to regulatory concerns. Monero's community has responded by emphasizing its legitimate use cases and commitment to privacy rights.

The Impact of Monero

Monero's introduction of advanced privacy technologies has ignited discussions about financial privacy, the importance of fungibility, and the evolving landscape of cryptocurrency regulations. Its adoption has grown within privacy-conscious communities and industries, demonstrating the demand for robust privacy features in digital transactions.

Broader Implications

Monero's journey underscores the value of privacy in an interconnected world. As the broader cryptocurrency ecosystem evolves, Monero's innovations serve as a reminder that the concept of pseudonymous transactions is a critical part of the future of digital finance. Monero's emphasis on privacy and fungibility has spurred further development of privacy coins and has fueled conversations about the balance between transparency and autonomy.

Conclusion

Monero's commitment to enhancing privacy and fungibility sets it apart in the cryptocurrency landscape. Its innovative use of ring signatures, stealth addresses, and Confidential Transactions has reshaped the way we perceive financial transactions in a digital age. Monero's story serves as a testament to the power of technology to empower individuals with the tools needed to protect their financial autonomy and personal privacy. As we continue our exploration of privacy coins and their impact, Monero's legacy reminds us of the ongoing quest for privacy and fungibility in a transparent world.

Zcash: Zero-Knowledge Proofs for Selective Transparency

In the realm of privacy coins, Zcash has carved a unique path by introducing a groundbreaking concept: zero-knowledge proofs. Unlike traditional cryptocurrencies that provide varying levels of privacy through pseudonymous transactions, Zcash offers a new approach that allows users to choose between transparent and shielded transactions. In this section, we delve into the story of Zcash's inception, the innovative application of zero-knowledge proofs, and its role in reshaping the narrative around financial privacy and selective transparency.

The Birth of Zcash

Launched in October 2016 by a team of researchers and developers, Zcash aimed to address the limitations of existing privacy coins by introducing a revolutionary cryptographic technique: zero-knowledge proofs. Zcash was the first cryptocurrency to offer optional privacy for transactions while still providing the option for transparent transactions similar to Bitcoin.

Zero-Knowledge Proofs: The Key Innovation

At the heart of Zcash's privacy technology lies zero-knowledge proofs. Zero-knowledge proofs allow one party (the prover) to prove to another party (the verifier) that a statement is true without revealing any additional information beyond the validity of the statement itself. This breakthrough cryptographic technique enables private transactions to occur on a public blockchain, introducing a new dimension of selective transparency.

Zcash's Two Types of Transactions

Zcash transactions come in two flavors: transparent and shielded. Transparent transactions are similar to Bitcoin transactions, providing basic transparency by displaying sender, receiver, and amount on the blockchain. In contrast, shielded transactions utilize zero-knowledge proofs to encrypt transaction details, obscuring sender, receiver, and amount while still being verifiable and validatable by network participants.

zk-SNARKs: Zero-Knowledge Succinct Non-Interactive Argument of Knowledge

The implementation of zero-knowledge proofs in Zcash relies on zk-SNARKs, a specific type of zero-knowledge proof. zk-SNARKs allow for the creation of compact and succinct proofs that verify the correctness of computations without revealing the inputs or intermediate steps. This efficient form of zero-knowledge proof made it possible for Zcash to enable shielded transactions without significantly bloating the blockchain.

Privacy with a Trade-Off

While shielded transactions offer unparalleled privacy, they do come with a trade-off. The cryptographic complexity required for zk-SNARKs means that shielded transactions are computationally more intensive, requiring greater computational resources and time compared to transparent transactions. This trade-off highlights the balance between privacy and efficiency that users must consider when choosing transaction types.

Privacy and Regulation

Zcash's approach to privacy through zero-knowledge proofs has sparked conversations about the balance between privacy and regulatory compliance. While Zcash enables optional privacy, there have been concerns that shielded transactions could be misused for illicit activities. Regulatory responses have varied, with some exchanges choosing to delist Zcash in an effort to comply with regulations.

Partnerships and Use Cases

Zcash's innovative technology and privacy features have attracted partnerships and collaborations with various organizations and institutions. Some applications include collaborations with blockchain analytics firms to develop tools for privacy-preserving audits and compliance checks. Zcash's potential extends beyond individual transactions to more complex applications involving confidential transactions and data privacy.

The Broader Impact

Zcash's introduction of zero-knowledge proofs and selective transparency has sparked conversations about the balance between privacy and the need for verifiability. It challenges traditional notions of financial transparency while introducing a flexible approach that empowers users to choose the level of privacy that aligns with their preferences and needs.

Conclusion

Zcash's groundbreaking use of zero-knowledge proofs for selective transparency marks a significant step forward in the evolution of privacy coins. Its approach offers a nuanced perspective on privacy, allowing users to navigate the trade-offs between transparency, efficiency, and confidentiality. As the cryptocurrency landscape continues to evolve, Zcash's legacy serves as a reminder of the innovative potential of cryptography to reshape how we engage with financial transactions and redefine the boundaries of privacy and transparency in the digital age.

Dash: A Focus on User Anonymity and Speed

Among the spectrum of privacy coins, Dash has carved its niche by placing emphasis on both transactional privacy and efficiency. Dash, short for "digital cash," was introduced with the goal of providing a seamless and user-friendly experience for both everyday transactions and privacy-conscious individuals. In this section, we delve into the genesis of Dash, its innovative features, including PrivateSend and InstantSend, and its impact on reshaping the narrative around user-centric privacy and transactional speed.

The Birth of Dash

Launched in January 2014 as a fork of Bitcoin, Dash aimed to improve upon the limitations of its predecessor by focusing on user experience, transaction speed, and privacy. Originally named "Darkcoin," the project rebranded to "Dash" in 2015 to reflect its focus on becoming digital cash—a cryptocurrency suitable for everyday transactions.

PrivateSend: Mixing for Anonymity

One of Dash's key privacy features is PrivateSend, a mixing mechanism designed to enhance transactional anonymity. PrivateSend works by combining multiple transactions into a single transaction with multiple inputs and outputs. This blending process makes it difficult to trace the origin and destination of funds, enhancing the privacy of transactions without revealing the sender's identity.

The Masternode Network

PrivateSend relies on Dash's unique masternode network, which consists of specialized nodes that provide enhanced services to the network. These masternodes facilitate the PrivateSend mixing process, as well as InstantSend transactions (discussed later). Masternodes play a crucial role in maintaining the network's privacy and speed features.

InstantSend: Near-Instant Confirmations

Dash also addresses the issue of transaction speed through its InstantSend feature. While Bitcoin transactions can take several minutes to confirm, InstantSend enables near-instant confirmations. InstantSend transactions are facilitated by masternodes, which lock and confirm transactions in seconds, making Dash suitable for point-of-sale transactions and other real-time use cases.

Decentralized Governance: Funding Development

Dash introduced an innovative governance system that allows network participants to propose and vote on improvements and projects. A portion of the block rewards generated by the network is allocated to fund approved proposals. This decentralized funding mechanism has enabled Dash's development to be driven by the community's priorities.

Evolution: The Path Forward

To further enhance its user experience and capabilities, Dash introduced Evolution—a project aimed at simplifying the cryptocurrency experience for mainstream users. Evolution envisions features such as usernames, contact lists, and a user-friendly interface, making Dash more accessible and intuitive for non-technical individuals.

Balancing Privacy and User Experience

Dash's unique focus on privacy and transaction speed aims to balance the need for anonymity with the practical requirements of everyday transactions. By offering features like PrivateSend and InstantSend, Dash caters to both privacy-conscious users seeking confidentiality and individuals looking for efficient and convenient digital cash solutions.

Challenges and Responses

While Dash's approach to privacy and efficiency has garnered attention, it has also faced criticism and challenges. Some critics argue that Dash's privacy features may not be as robust as those of other privacy coins, raising concerns about the potential for traceability. Dash's community has responded by emphasizing the importance of informed usage and proper configuration of privacy features.

Impact and Adoption

Dash's user-centric approach has led to adoption in various industries, including merchant services, remittances, and point-of-sale solutions. Its focus on providing a seamless user experience and incorporating user feedback has contributed to its popularity in regions with specific needs for fast and private transactions.

Broader Implications

Dash's journey in combining privacy and speed highlights the potential for cryptocurrencies to offer practical solutions to real-world problems. Its user-friendly features have paved the way for cryptocurrency adoption beyond the tech-savvy demographic, showcasing the power of innovation in reshaping digital financial interactions.

Conclusion

Dash's emphasis on user anonymity and speed has positioned it as a versatile cryptocurrency that seeks to address both the privacy concerns of individuals and the practical requirements of everyday transactions. Its unique approach to mixing and instant confirmations has set a precedent for user-centric design within the cryptocurrency space. As we explore the world of privacy coins and their impact, Dash's legacy reminds us that cryptocurrencies can serve as tools for empowerment and provide innovative solutions to long-standing financial challenges.

Chapter 4: Blockchain Beyond Currency
Blockchain Applications: Beyond Financial Transactions

The emergence of blockchain technology has transcended its initial role as the foundation for cryptocurrencies. As the potential of this revolutionary technology became evident, innovators began exploring its application in various industries beyond finance. This chapter delves into the diverse and transformative applications of blockchain technology, showcasing how it has disrupted traditional systems, introduced new levels of transparency and security, and revolutionized industries beyond financial transactions.

The Evolution of Blockchain Beyond Currency

While blockchain technology's first mainstream application was in cryptocurrencies like Bitcoin, its underlying principles soon led to the realization that its potential extended far beyond financial transactions. This shift in focus gave birth to a wide array of blockchain applications that aimed to solve longstanding challenges in different sectors.

Decentralized Identity and Digital Identity Management

Blockchain's immutability and security features have made it an ideal candidate for creating decentralized and tamper-proof identity systems. By allowing individuals to have control over their personal data and providing verifiable proofs of identity without relying on central authorities, blockchain-based identity systems offer enhanced security, privacy, and interoperability.

Supply Chain Management and Traceability

Blockchain has transformed supply chain management by creating transparent and tamper-proof records of every step in a product's journey. This enables stakeholders to track products from their origin to the end consumer, reducing fraud, ensuring product authenticity, and enhancing accountability. The technology has particularly proven valuable in industries like food, luxury goods, and pharmaceuticals.

Digital Ownership and Non-Fungible Tokens (NFTs)

Non-Fungible Tokens (NFTs) have captured global attention as blockchain-based assets that represent ownership of unique items, such as digital art, collectibles, and virtual real estate. By introducing verifiable scarcity and provenance, NFTs revolutionize digital ownership and allow creators to monetize their work in new and innovative ways.

Smart Contracts and Decentralized Applications (dApps)

Ethereum's introduction of smart contracts has paved the way for the development of decentralized applications (dApps) that execute code based on predefined conditions. These dApps, ranging from decentralized finance (DeFi) protocols to prediction markets, aim to disrupt traditional industries by eliminating intermediaries, automating processes, and offering new ways to interact with digital services.

Voting and Governance

Blockchain technology has the potential to revolutionize voting systems by providing a tamper-proof and transparent platform for conducting elections. By enabling voters to verify their votes and ensuring the integrity of the electoral process, blockchain-based voting systems address concerns about fraud and manipulation in traditional voting systems.

Healthcare and Data Sharing

Blockchain's secure and interoperable nature makes it an ideal solution for healthcare data management. It allows patients to have control over their health records while enabling authorized parties to access relevant information securely. This enhances patient privacy and facilitates data sharing between healthcare providers, improving patient care and reducing medical errors.

Challenges and Considerations

While the potential of blockchain applications is vast, challenges such as scalability, interoperability, regulatory concerns, and energy consumption must be addressed. Balancing the advantages of decentralization with the practical needs of different industries poses ongoing challenges that require collaboration between technology developers, regulators, and industry stakeholders.

Impact and Future Prospects

The impact of blockchain technology beyond financial transactions has been transformative, paving the way for new business models, increasing transparency, and empowering individuals. As the technology continues to evolve, blockchain applications are expected to play a significant role in reshaping industries, fostering innovation, and fostering a new era of decentralized and secure interactions.

Conclusion

The expansion of blockchain technology beyond currency signifies a shift towards decentralized, transparent, and tamper-proof systems across various sectors. From identity management to supply chain tracking, blockchain's potential to disrupt traditional models and create new possibilities is undeniable. As blockchain applications continue to evolve and integrate into daily life, the underlying principles of decentralization, transparency, and security will continue to drive innovation and redefine the way we interact with information, services, and assets.

Decentralized Finance (DeFi): Smart Contracts in Finance

The rise of blockchain technology has paved the way for the evolution of traditional financial systems into a more open, transparent, and decentralized ecosystem known as Decentralized Finance (DeFi). At the heart of this transformation are smart contracts, self-executing code on the blockchain that enable the creation of various financial instruments and services. This section explores the emergence of DeFi, the role of smart contracts, and how they are reshaping the financial landscape.

The Birth of DeFi

Decentralized Finance, often referred to as DeFi, represents a paradigm shift in the financial industry. It aims to democratize access to financial services by leveraging blockchain technology and removing intermediaries, such as banks and traditional financial institutions. DeFi projects are built on the principles of transparency, security, and inclusivity, allowing individuals to participate in financial activities without relying on centralized authorities.

Smart Contracts: The Foundation of DeFi

At the core of DeFi are smart contracts—autonomous pieces of code that execute predefined actions when specific conditions are met. Smart contracts enable the creation of a wide range of financial products and services, including lending, borrowing, trading, asset management, derivatives, and more. These contracts are executed automatically and without the need for intermediaries, ensuring efficiency and transparency.

Lending and Borrowing Protocols

DeFi lending platforms allow users to lend their cryptocurrencies and earn interest, while borrowers can access loans without the need for traditional credit checks. Smart contracts facilitate the lending process by automatically managing collateral and interest payments. These platforms offer a decentralized alternative to traditional banking services.

Decentralized Exchanges (DEXs)

Decentralized exchanges enable peer-to-peer trading of cryptocurrencies without relying on a central authority. They utilize smart contracts to execute trades and manage order books. DEXs provide greater control over assets and reduce the risks associated with centralized exchanges, such as hacking and custody concerns.

Automated Market Makers (AMMs)

AMMs are a subset of decentralized exchanges that use algorithms and smart contracts to facilitate trading. They replace traditional order books with liquidity pools, allowing users to trade directly against these pools. AMMs have gained popularity for their simplicity and accessibility.

Yield Farming and Liquidity Mining

Yield farming involves providing liquidity to DeFi protocols in exchange for rewards. Users contribute their assets to liquidity pools, and in return, they receive fees and tokens. Liquidity mining takes this concept further by incentivizing users to provide liquidity to specific pairs, driving liquidity to particular markets.

Stablecoins and Synthetic Assets

Stablecoins are blockchain-based digital assets designed to maintain a stable value, often pegged to traditional fiat currencies. They serve as a bridge between the traditional financial world and the decentralized ecosystem. Synthetic assets, on the other hand, replicate the value of real-world assets like stocks, commodities, and even traditional financial instruments like futures and options.

Challenges and Opportunities

Despite the promise of DeFi, challenges remain. These include smart contract vulnerabilities, regulatory uncertainties, scalability concerns, and the risk of market manipulation. Additionally, while DeFi aims to democratize finance, there are challenges related to accessibility, user education, and the potential for wealth concentration.

The Growing DeFi Ecosystem

The DeFi ecosystem is a dynamic and rapidly evolving space. It has witnessed explosive growth in terms of Total Value Locked (TVL), user adoption, and the number of projects. However, with this growth come risks and uncertainties, which underscore the importance of responsible innovation and risk management.

Future Outlook

DeFi has the potential to revolutionize traditional finance by offering accessible, transparent, and decentralized alternatives to traditional financial services. As the technology matures, challenges are being addressed through improvements in smart contract security, interoperability, and scalability solutions. The future of DeFi holds the promise of an open and inclusive financial ecosystem that empowers individuals and transforms global finance.

Conclusion

Decentralized Finance, driven by the power of smart contracts, is reshaping the financial industry by creating a more inclusive and open ecosystem. The integration of blockchain technology and financial services has the potential to disrupt traditional models, democratize access, and redefine the way individuals engage with financial products and services. As the DeFi space continues to evolve, it reflects the broader shift towards decentralized systems that empower users and challenge traditional financial paradigms.

Non-Fungible Tokens (NFTs): Digital Collectibles and Ownership

The advent of blockchain technology has given rise to a revolutionary concept known as Non-Fungible Tokens (NFTs), which are redefining digital ownership and creating a new economy for digital assets. NFTs represent unique and indivisible digital items that can range from digital art to virtual real estate and even moments in time. This section explores the emergence of NFTs, their underlying technology, and their profound impact on the worlds of art, entertainment, gaming, and beyond.

The Rise of NFTs

NFTs have transformed the way we perceive digital ownership. Unlike fungible cryptocurrencies like Bitcoin or Ethereum, NFTs represent ownership of distinct, non-interchangeable digital items. This distinction makes them suitable for representing one-of-a-kind assets in the digital realm.

Token Standards and Technology

The Ethereum blockchain played a pivotal role in popularizing NFTs, primarily through its ERC-721 token standard. This standard introduced a framework for creating unique tokens, each with its own metadata and properties. ERC-1155, another token standard, allows for both fungible and non-fungible tokens to coexist within the same smart contract, providing greater flexibility.

Digital Art: Redefining Creativity and Ownership

NFTs have sparked a revolution in the art world by enabling artists to tokenize their creations as digital art. Digital artists can now monetize their work by selling NFTs, allowing collectors to own a unique piece of digital art with provable ownership and provenance. This innovation challenges traditional notions of art ownership and access.

Virtual Real Estate and Digital Worlds

NFTs have extended their reach into virtual reality and metaverse environments, where ownership of virtual real estate and digital items becomes a reality. Virtual worlds built on blockchain platforms like Decentraland and The Sandbox allow users to buy, sell, and build on NFT-based land parcels, paving the way for a new era of digital real estate.

Gaming: NFTs in the Gaming Industry

The gaming industry has embraced NFTs, allowing players to own and trade in-game assets as NFTs. This introduces true ownership and transferability of in-game items, creating new opportunities for players to monetize their gaming experiences. NFTs are also fostering the development of play-to-earn models, where players can earn income through their in-game activities.

Celebrities, Sports, and Tokenized Moments

Celebrities and sports figures are leveraging NFTs to tokenize moments and experiences. Iconic moments from sports events, music performances, and other celebrity appearances are being turned into NFTs, allowing fans to own a piece of history and interact with their idols in unprecedented ways.

Challenges and Considerations

While the NFT space is brimming with innovation, challenges remain. Scalability concerns, environmental impact, copyright issues, and potential market oversaturation are among the challenges that must be addressed as the NFT ecosystem continues to grow.

Impact and Cultural Shift

NFTs have triggered a cultural shift in how we value and perceive digital content and ownership. The concept of digital scarcity introduced by NFTs is challenging the digital abundance paradigm of the internet, pushing the boundaries of what can be owned, shared, and monetized in the digital realm.

Economic Implications and Future Prospects

NFTs have created new economic models, enabling creators and collectors to monetize digital assets in unprecedented ways. The NFT ecosystem is evolving beyond speculation to focus on building sustainable value, infrastructure, and platforms that empower creators and users alike.

Conclusion

Non-Fungible Tokens (NFTs) represent a groundbreaking concept that transcends traditional notions of ownership and value in the digital realm. The intersection of blockchain technology, creativity, and ownership has given rise to a vibrant ecosystem that spans art, entertainment, gaming, and beyond. As NFTs continue to redefine how we interact with digital assets, they underscore the transformative power of blockchain technology in reshaping our relationship with digital content and ownership in a rapidly evolving digital age.

Supply Chain Management: Transparency and Traceability

Blockchain technology has ushered in a new era of transparency and traceability in supply chain management, revolutionizing how products are tracked, verified, and authenticated throughout their journey from production to consumption. This section delves into the transformative impact of blockchain on supply chain management, exploring its applications in various industries, the challenges it addresses, and its potential to reshape global trade and consumer confidence.

The Challenge of Supply Chain Opacity

Supply chains are complex networks involving multiple stakeholders, geographical locations, and processes. The lack of transparency and the risk of information asymmetry have led to challenges such as counterfeit products, ethical concerns, and inefficiencies. Blockchain technology offers a solution by providing an immutable, transparent, and tamper-proof record of every step in the supply chain.

Blockchain's Role in Supply Chain Management

Blockchain's distributed ledger technology offers a platform for creating a trustworthy and verifiable record of supply chain transactions and events. Each transaction is cryptographically linked, ensuring that once data is recorded, it cannot be altered without detection. This creates a single source of truth that all participants can trust, fostering collaboration and accountability.

Enhancing Transparency and Traceability

Blockchain's impact on supply chain management can be summarized in two main aspects: transparency and traceability.

Transparency: Blockchain enables real-time visibility into supply chain processes. This transparency is essential for verifying the authenticity of products, ensuring compliance with regulations, and addressing ethical concerns such as fair labor practices and environmental sustainability.

Traceability: The ability to trace the origin, movement, and transformation of products is crucial for industries such as agriculture, pharmaceuticals, and luxury goods. Blockchain's immutable records enable quick and accurate tracing of goods, reducing the time required to identify and address issues such as recalls or contamination.

Applications in Various Industries

Food and Agriculture: Blockchain is being used to track the journey of food products from farm to table. This ensures food safety, reduces waste, and enables consumers to make informed choices about the products they purchase.

Pharmaceuticals: In the pharmaceutical industry, blockchain helps combat counterfeit drugs by providing a tamper-proof record of the drug's journey, verifying its authenticity, and improving patient safety.

Luxury Goods: Blockchain verifies the authenticity and provenance of luxury goods, reducing the risk of purchasing counterfeit items and protecting brand reputation.

Challenges Addressed by Blockchain

Counterfeit Prevention: Counterfeit products cost industries billions of dollars annually. Blockchain's transparent and tamper-proof records help verify the authenticity of products, protecting consumers and brands.

Ethical Sourcing: Blockchain can trace the origin of raw materials, ensuring that products are sourced ethically and in compliance with labor and environmental regulations.

Regulatory Compliance: Industries face stringent regulations, and ensuring compliance across the supply chain can be challenging. Blockchain provides a verifiable record of compliance, simplifying audits and reducing regulatory risks.

Dispute Resolution: Disputes often arise due to discrepancies in supply chain records. Blockchain's accurate and immutable records facilitate quick and fair dispute resolution.

Potential to Reshape Global Trade

Blockchain's impact on supply chain management extends beyond individual industries. It has the potential to reshape global trade by streamlining cross-border transactions, reducing paperwork, and enhancing trust between international trading partners.

Challenges and Considerations

While blockchain offers significant benefits, challenges such as scalability, interoperability, data privacy, and standardization need to be addressed for widespread adoption. Integration with legacy systems and convincing stakeholders to share data on a transparent platform can also pose challenges.

Collaboration and Ecosystem Building

Successful implementation of blockchain in supply chain management requires collaboration among stakeholders across the supply chain. The development of industry-specific consortia, partnerships, and standards is crucial to creating a cohesive ecosystem.

Future Prospects

As blockchain technology matures and addresses challenges, its impact on supply chain management is expected to deepen. The development of interoperable blockchain networks and the integration of Internet of Things (IoT) devices offer opportunities for further innovation and optimization.

Conclusion

Blockchain's application in supply chain management is ushering in a new era of transparency, traceability, and accountability. By leveraging its inherent features of immutability and transparency, blockchain technology is addressing challenges related to counterfeit products, ethical concerns, regulatory compliance, and more. As industries embrace blockchain to create more reliable and efficient supply chains, the technology's potential to reshape global trade and consumer confidence becomes increasingly evident.

Chapter 5: Scalability and Interoperability

Scaling Challenges: Addressing the Limitations of Blockchain

Blockchain technology has demonstrated immense potential to revolutionize industries, but its widespread adoption has been hindered by inherent limitations, particularly in scalability. As more applications and users join blockchain networks, concerns about transaction speed, capacity, and efficiency have become prominent. This section delves into the challenges posed by scalability in blockchain networks, the various solutions proposed to address them, and the ongoing efforts to achieve greater scalability while maintaining the principles of decentralization and security.

The Scalability Paradox

The promise of decentralized systems comes with a trade-off: as more users participate in a blockchain network, the consensus process becomes slower and resource-intensive. This challenge is commonly referred to as the scalability paradox, where the decentralized nature of blockchains inherently hampers their ability to handle a large number of transactions in a timely and efficient manner.

Limitations of Traditional Blockchains

Most early blockchain networks, including Bitcoin and Ethereum, rely on a consensus mechanism called Proof of Work (PoW). While PoW ensures security, it also limits the number of transactions that can be processed within a given time frame. The block size, block interval, and validation process contribute to the scalability challenge, resulting in high fees during periods of network congestion.

Increasing Block Size and Frequency

One approach to addressing scalability is to increase the block size or reduce the block interval. However, this approach faces challenges related to network synchronization, storage requirements, and centralization risks. Larger blocks can lead to longer validation times and higher resource demands for network participants.

Layer 2 Solutions: Off-Chain Scalability

Layer 2 solutions aim to achieve scalability by processing transactions off-chain while still settling the final outcome on the main blockchain. The Lightning Network for Bitcoin and similar solutions for Ethereum, such as Optimistic Rollups, enable rapid and low-cost transactions by creating payment channels or aggregating transactions before committing them to the main blockchain.

Sharding: Parallel Processing

Sharding is a technique that involves splitting the blockchain network into smaller, interconnected shards, each capable of processing transactions independently. Shards can run in parallel, significantly increasing the network's capacity and throughput. Ethereum's proposed Ethereum 2.0 upgrade includes a sharding mechanism to enhance scalability.

Interoperability and Cross-Chain Communication

As blockchain networks proliferate, the issue of interoperability arises. Different blockchains often operate in isolation, preventing seamless communication and data sharing. Cross-chain solutions, such as interoperability protocols and bridges, aim to enable the exchange of assets and data between different blockchains.

Sidechains: Specialized Chains

Sidechains are separate blockchains connected to a main blockchain through a two-way peg mechanism. They allow for the execution of specific use cases or applications with their own rules and consensus mechanisms while maintaining compatibility with the main blockchain. Sidechains enhance scalability by offloading transactions and computation from the main chain.

State Channels: Off-Chain State

State channels enable participants to conduct multiple transactions off-chain while periodically updating the main blockchain with the final state. These channels can be used for various purposes, from micropayments to gaming. State channels address the scalability issue by reducing the need for on-chain transactions.

Challenges and Considerations

While these solutions hold promise, challenges remain. Interoperability between different scaling solutions, security risks, decentralization trade-offs, and the need for network upgrades are among the considerations that must be carefully navigated.

Balancing Scalability with Decentralization

Achieving scalability while maintaining decentralization and security is a delicate balancing act. While scalability solutions can enhance transaction throughput, they must not compromise the core principles of blockchain technology, which include distributed consensus and trustlessness.

The Path Forward: Collaboration and Innovation

The blockchain community is actively collaborating to develop and implement scalable solutions that can cater to diverse use cases. The integration of multiple approaches, the exploration of new consensus mechanisms, and the refinement of existing protocols are critical to building a scalable blockchain ecosystem.

Conclusion

Scalability remains a central challenge for blockchain technology as it strives to accommodate the demands of a global user base and an expanding array of applications. The pursuit of solutions to the scalability paradox is a testament to the innovative spirit of the blockchain community. As the technology continues to evolve, finding the right balance between scalability, decentralization, and security will be key to unlocking the full potential of blockchain networks across industries and sectors.

Layer 2 Solutions: Lightning Network and Payment Channels

The growth of blockchain technology has brought to light the pressing need for solutions that address its scalability challenges. Among these solutions, Layer 2 protocols have emerged as a promising avenue to enhance transaction throughput and efficiency while maintaining the decentralization and security that are at the core of blockchain's value proposition. This section delves into the concept of Layer 2 solutions, focusing on the Lightning Network and payment channels as prominent examples, exploring their architecture, benefits, challenges, and the transformative potential they hold for the future of blockchain scalability.

Understanding Layer 2 Solutions

Layer 2 solutions operate "on top" of existing blockchains, building an additional layer that processes transactions and interactions off-chain, and subsequently settles them on the main blockchain. These solutions aim to mitigate the scalability limitations inherent in the consensus mechanisms of most major blockchains, enabling faster and cheaper transactions.

The Lightning Network: A Scalability Breakthrough

The Lightning Network is a prominent example of a Layer 2 solution, primarily designed to address Bitcoin's scalability challenges. It introduces a network of payment channels that enable participants to conduct transactions off-chain, only settling the final result on the Bitcoin blockchain. The Lightning Network's architecture, consisting of payment channels, nodes, and multi-signature wallets, creates a decentralized and efficient network for microtransactions.

Payment Channels: Enabling Off-Chain Transactions

Payment channels are at the heart of the Lightning Network. They are essentially multi-signature wallets that allow users to lock up a certain amount of cryptocurrency, enabling them to send and receive payments off-chain. The parties involved can conduct an unlimited number of transactions within the channel without burdening the main blockchain.

Benefits of the Lightning Network

- Scalability: The Lightning Network's off-chain nature significantly increases the number of transactions that can be processed in a short period of time, alleviating congestion on the main blockchain.

- Speed: Transactions conducted on the Lightning Network are near-instantaneous, enabling real-time microtransactions that are impractical on-chain due to confirmation times.

- Cost Efficiency: Lightning Network transactions come with lower fees compared to on-chain transactions, making small-value transactions economically viable.

- Privacy: The off-chain nature of Lightning Network transactions enhances privacy, as they do not need to be recorded on the public blockchain.

- Microtransactions and Use Cases: The Lightning Network enables micropayments and use cases such as content monetization, tipping, gaming, and streaming services, which rely on rapid and low-cost transactions.

Challenges and Considerations

While the Lightning Network offers significant advantages, it also faces challenges that need to be addressed for its widespread adoption:

- Routing Challenges: Routing payments through a network of nodes can sometimes lead to inefficiencies and complexities, requiring optimization.

- Channel Management: Participants need to actively manage their channels, ensuring that they have enough funds available for transactions.

- Security and Watchtowers: Ensuring the security of Lightning Network channels and preventing fraudulent behavior, such as channel closure attempts, requires the deployment of watchtowers.

- Interoperability and Network Effects: Achieving interoperability between different implementations of the Lightning Network and building a robust network of nodes are essential for its success.

The Future of Layer 2 Solutions

The Lightning Network has paved the way for further exploration and development of Layer 2 solutions in various blockchain ecosystems. Ethereum is also exploring similar Layer 2 solutions, such as Optimistic Rollups and zk-rollups, to enhance scalability and reduce congestion.

Use Cases Beyond Payments

While the Lightning Network's primary focus is on enabling fast and cheap transactions, its underlying technology has potential applications beyond payments. Ideas like decentralized finance (DeFi) protocols, decentralized applications (dApps), and even secure messaging systems can benefit from the off-chain capabilities provided by the Lightning Network.

Conclusion

Layer 2 solutions, exemplified by the Lightning Network, represent a crucial step toward solving blockchain's scalability challenges. These solutions offer a way to enhance transaction throughput, reduce fees, and enable rapid micropayments while preserving the core principles of decentralization and security. The ongoing development, optimization, and adoption of Layer 2 solutions will likely play a pivotal role in shaping the future of blockchain technology, allowing it to accommodate the demands of a global user base and a wide array of applications.

Interoperability: Bridging Different Blockchains

The proliferation of blockchain networks has resulted in a fragmented landscape, where various blockchains operate independently with limited communication between them. Interoperability, the ability for different blockchains to seamlessly exchange information and value, has emerged as a critical solution to address this fragmentation. This section explores the concept of interoperability, its importance, the challenges it aims to solve, and the innovative approaches and technologies being developed to bridge different blockchains and unlock their full potential.

The Need for Interoperability

As blockchain technology has evolved, numerous blockchains with distinct features, consensus mechanisms, and use cases have emerged. However, the lack of interoperability between these blockchains has hindered their ability to work together cohesively and realize their full potential. Interoperability is essential to overcome this fragmentation and create a unified blockchain ecosystem.

Challenges of Interoperability

Interoperability poses several challenges that must be addressed to create effective cross-chain communication:

- Consensus and Security: Different blockchains may use varying consensus mechanisms, introducing challenges in maintaining security and trust when transferring assets or information between them.

- Data Standardization: Ensuring uniform data standards and formatting across different blockchains is crucial to enable seamless communication.

- Atomic Swaps: Atomic swaps allow direct exchange of assets across different blockchains without the need for intermediaries, but technical complexities and potential vulnerabilities need to be managed.

- Decentralization: Achieving interoperability without sacrificing the decentralization and security of individual blockchains is a complex task.

Approaches to Interoperability

Various approaches and technologies are being developed to enable interoperability between different blockchains:

- Cross-Chain Platforms: Cross-chain platforms like Polkadot and Cosmos provide frameworks for creating interconnected blockchain networks, allowing assets and data to move between chains.

- Blockchain Bridges: Blockchain bridges are smart contracts or protocols that facilitate the movement of assets between different blockchains. These bridges ensure security and trust during cross-chain transactions.

- Wrapped Tokens: Wrapped tokens represent assets from one blockchain on another blockchain through a trusted intermediary. This enables the transfer of value between different blockchains while maintaining transparency.

- Interoperability Protocols: Interoperability protocols like Interledger and Atomic Multi-Path Payments (AMP) focus on enabling cross-chain value transfer while addressing challenges like scalability and transaction privacy.

- Sidechains and Pegging Mechanisms: Sidechains are separate blockchains linked to a main blockchain, allowing assets to be moved between them. Pegging mechanisms ensure that assets on the sidechain are backed by an equivalent amount of assets on the main chain.

Real-World Applications

Interoperability has the potential to revolutionize various industries:

- Finance: Interoperable blockchains can facilitate cross-border payments, tokenized assets, and decentralized finance (DeFi) protocols that operate seamlessly across different chains.

- Supply Chain Management: Different blockchains can collaborate to create a unified supply chain network, enabling transparent tracking of goods and data across multiple stages.

- Healthcare: Secure sharing of patient data across different healthcare systems and providers can be achieved through interoperable blockchain networks.

- IoT and Smart Cities: Interconnected blockchain networks can enable secure data sharing and coordination among Internet of Things (IoT) devices and smart city infrastructure.

The Future of Interoperability

Interoperability is a key enabler of the blockchain ecosystem's growth and maturation. As technology advances, achieving seamless interoperability will involve addressing technical, security, and governance challenges.

Collaboration and Standardization

Creating a truly interoperable blockchain ecosystem requires collaboration among projects, organizations, and developers. Standardization of protocols and data formats is crucial for ensuring compatibility between different blockchains.

Conclusion

Interoperability holds the key to realizing the full potential of blockchain technology. By enabling different blockchains to communicate, exchange value, and collaborate seamlessly, interoperability addresses the fragmentation that has held back the blockchain ecosystem. As the development of interoperability technologies and standards continues, the vision of a unified blockchain network becomes ever closer to reality, promising greater efficiency, innovation, and value for industries and users worldwide.

The Future of Scalability: Sharding and Sidechains

As blockchain technology continues to evolve, the need for scalable solutions becomes increasingly pressing. Sharding and sidechains represent two innovative approaches that hold the promise of significantly enhancing blockchain scalability while maintaining decentralization and security. This section explores the concepts of sharding and sidechains, their potential benefits, challenges, and the implications they could have for the future of blockchain technology and its widespread adoption.

Sharding: A Paradigm Shift in Scalability

Sharding introduces a groundbreaking paradigm shift in blockchain scalability. Traditionally, every node in a blockchain network validates and stores the entire transaction history, which can lead to bottlenecks and inefficiencies. Sharding aims to divide the network into smaller, interconnected shards, allowing multiple transactions to be processed in parallel across these shards.

How Sharding Works

In a sharded blockchain network, each shard is responsible for processing a subset of transactions. This enables the network to handle a higher throughput of transactions simultaneously. Sharding involves:

- State Partitioning: The network's state, including user balances and smart contracts, is divided into shards.

- Transaction Processing: Each shard processes its assigned transactions independently, leveraging parallel processing capabilities.

- Cross-Shard Communication: Shards can communicate with each other when transactions involve multiple shards, ensuring that data and value can move between them.

Benefits of Sharding

- Scalability: Sharding significantly increases the transaction throughput of the blockchain network, addressing one of the major limitations of existing blockchains.

- Efficiency: Parallel processing allows for faster confirmation times and reduced congestion during high demand periods.

- Resource Efficiency: Shards require fewer resources to validate transactions, making blockchain participation more accessible.

- Decentralization: Sharding can help maintain a balance between decentralization and scalability by enabling more participants to run nodes.

Challenges and Considerations

- Cross-Shard Communication: Ensuring efficient cross-shard communication without compromising security is a complex challenge.

- Data Availability: Shards need access to the state data of other shards to verify transactions, necessitating mechanisms for data availability.

- Security and Consensus: Achieving consensus within individual shards while ensuring network-wide security remains a challenge.

- Network Upgrades: Implementing sharding often requires network upgrades and changes to existing protocols, which can be complex and risky.

Sidechains: Expanding the Blockchain Universe

Sidechains provide another avenue for enhancing blockchain scalability while maintaining interoperability. A sidechain is a separate blockchain connected to the main blockchain, allowing assets and data to move between them. Sidechains enable the development of specialized applications without congesting the main blockchain.

How Sidechains Work

Sidechains operate alongside the main blockchain, with a two-way peg mechanism connecting them. This mechanism allows users to lock assets on the main chain and mint equivalent assets on the sidechain. Users can then conduct transactions on the sidechain, benefiting from its features before moving assets back to the main chain.

Benefits of Sidechains

- Scalability: Sidechains offload transactions and computation from the main blockchain, enhancing overall scalability.

- Customizability: Developers can create sidechains with specific use cases or features tailored to their needs.

- Reduced Congestion: Popular applications or use cases can be moved to sidechains, reducing congestion on the main chain.

- Innovation: Sidechains encourage experimentation and innovation by providing a sandbox environment for new ideas.

Challenges and Considerations

- Security and Trust: Ensuring the security and trust of assets moved between the main chain and sidechains is crucial.

- Decentralization: Maintaining a balance between decentralization and security while using sidechains requires careful design.

- Two-Way Peg Mechanism: The mechanism for locking and unlocking assets between the main chain and sidechain must be secure and reliable.

The Future Landscape

Both sharding and sidechains offer unique approaches to enhancing blockchain scalability. Their coexistence and potential synergy can shape the future landscape of blockchain technology:

- Hybrid Approaches: Some blockchain projects are exploring hybrid approaches that combine sharding and sidechains to achieve optimal scalability.

- Specialized Use Cases: Sidechains can accommodate specialized use cases, while sharding addresses the broader need for high throughput.

- Research and Development: Continuous research and development are essential to address the challenges associated with both sharding and sidechains.

Conclusion

Sharding and sidechains represent the next frontier in blockchain scalability. While they introduce new complexities and challenges, their potential benefits are substantial. These innovative approaches hold the promise of unlocking greater transaction throughput, expanding the range of applications that can be built on blockchain technology, and ultimately enabling broader adoption across industries. As research, development, and experimentation in these areas continue, sharding and sidechains could play a transformative role in shaping the future of blockchain technology.

Chapter 6: Regulation and Challenges
Government Responses: Regulations and Legal Frameworks

The rise of cryptocurrencies and blockchain technology has triggered a global conversation about the need for regulatory frameworks to address the opportunities and challenges they present. Governments and regulatory bodies worldwide are grappling with how to strike a balance between fostering innovation and ensuring consumer protection, financial stability, and the prevention of illicit activities. This section delves into the complex landscape of government responses to cryptocurrencies, exploring the motivations behind regulations, the approaches taken by different countries, and the potential impact on the future of blockchain technology and its adoption.

Understanding the Regulatory Landscape

Governments have been responding to the emergence of cryptocurrencies and blockchain technology with varying degrees of enthusiasm, skepticism, and caution. The regulatory landscape is characterized by diverse perspectives, and each jurisdiction is crafting its own approach to address the unique opportunities and challenges presented by these technologies.

Motivations for Regulations

Governments' motivations for regulating cryptocurrencies and blockchain technology often revolve around several key factors:

- Consumer Protection: Ensuring the safety and rights of consumers who engage in cryptocurrency transactions and investments.

- Financial Stability: Mitigating risks to the broader financial system posed by the use of cryptocurrencies, such as potential systemic risks and market manipulation.

- Preventing Illicit Activities: Curbing money laundering, terrorist financing, and other illicit activities that could be facilitated by cryptocurrencies' pseudonymous nature.

- Taxation and Reporting: Establishing mechanisms to tax cryptocurrency transactions and require reporting to ensure compliance with tax obligations.

- Innovation and Economic Growth: Balancing regulatory oversight with fostering innovation and supporting the growth of the blockchain industry within the country.

Approaches to Regulation

The approaches governments take to regulate cryptocurrencies and blockchain technology can be broadly categorized into several models:

- Prohibition: Some countries have outright banned cryptocurrencies, citing concerns about consumer protection, financial stability, and potential criminal activities.

- Licensing and Registration: Other jurisdictions require businesses engaged in cryptocurrency-related activities to obtain licenses or register with regulatory bodies.

- Consumer Warnings: Some governments have opted for issuing consumer warnings to inform the public about the risks associated with cryptocurrencies and encourage informed decision-making.

- Establishing Regulatory Frameworks: Many countries are working on comprehensive regulatory frameworks that provide clarity on how cryptocurrencies and blockchain technology should be treated legally.

Case Studies: Regulatory Approaches

- United States: The U.S. has adopted a piecemeal approach, with regulatory bodies like the SEC and CFTC treating cryptocurrencies as securities or commodities. The landscape is evolving, with various agencies providing guidance on different aspects of the technology.

- European Union: The EU is working to establish a comprehensive regulatory framework through initiatives like the Fifth Anti-Money Laundering Directive (5AMLD) and the Markets in Crypto-Assets Regulation (MiCA).

- Japan: Japan was one of the first countries to officially recognize cryptocurrencies as a legal form of payment. The country's approach involves licensing cryptocurrency exchanges and establishing consumer protection measures.

- China: China has taken a strict stance, banning initial coin offerings (ICOs), cryptocurrency exchanges, and mining activities due to concerns about financial stability and capital outflows.

Challenges and Considerations

The regulatory landscape is complex and rife with challenges:

- Global Coordination: Cryptocurrencies are inherently global, making coordination between countries vital to address cross-border challenges.

- Innovation and Stifling Growth: Overregulation could stifle innovation and drive businesses to more favorable jurisdictions.

- Technology Neutrality: Regulators need to ensure that regulations are technology-neutral and adaptable to the rapidly evolving blockchain landscape.

- Consumer Education: Governments must prioritize educating consumers about the risks and benefits of cryptocurrencies to prevent uninformed decision-making.

Balancing Act: Striking the Right Balance

Finding the right balance between regulation and innovation is a delicate challenge. Too much regulation can stifle innovation, while too little can lead to consumer harm and financial instability. Regulatory sandboxes, pilot programs, and close collaboration between regulators, industry players, and researchers can help strike this balance.

Impact on the Future of Blockchain Technology

The regulatory environment will play a pivotal role in shaping the future of blockchain technology:

- Mainstream Adoption: Clear and favorable regulations can encourage mainstream adoption of cryptocurrencies and blockchain applications.

- Innovation Hubs: Countries with supportive regulatory environments may become innovation hubs for the blockchain industry.

- Global Standardization: The evolution of global standards and norms for blockchain regulation will impact international collaborations and cross-border transactions.

Conclusion

Government responses to cryptocurrencies and blockchain technology are crucial factors that will shape the trajectory of the technology's adoption and impact. Striking the right balance between innovation, consumer protection, financial stability, and the prevention of illicit activities is a complex challenge that requires collaboration between governments, industry stakeholders, and the broader public. As the regulatory landscape continues to evolve, its impact on the growth, innovation, and global adoption of blockchain technology will become increasingly evident.

Security and Hacks: Protecting Digital Assets

As the adoption of cryptocurrencies and blockchain technology has grown, so has the prominence of security concerns and the vulnerability of digital assets to various forms of cyberattacks. Protecting these assets from theft, hacks, and malicious activities has become a critical challenge for individuals, businesses, and the entire blockchain ecosystem. This section explores the multifaceted landscape of security in the blockchain realm, delving into common attack vectors, best practices for safeguarding digital assets, and the ongoing efforts to enhance security measures within the blockchain ecosystem.

The Complexity of Security Challenges

Blockchain technology and cryptocurrencies have introduced new security paradigms and risks that differ from those in traditional financial systems. Key security challenges include:

- Private Key Management: The cornerstone of blockchain security lies in the management of private keys, which are used to sign transactions and control access to digital assets.

- Attack Vectors: Malicious actors exploit vulnerabilities in various layers of the blockchain ecosystem, including wallet applications, exchanges, smart contracts, and even the consensus mechanism.

- Regulatory Compliance: Security measures must also adhere to regulatory requirements, which vary by jurisdiction.

Common Security Risks and Attacks

- Phishing Attacks: Fraudulent websites, emails, or messages lure users into revealing their private keys or personal information.

- Exchange Hacks: Cryptocurrency exchanges have been prime targets for hackers seeking to steal large amounts of digital assets.

- Wallet Vulnerabilities: Weaknesses in software wallets or poor private key management can lead to unauthorized access.

- Smart Contract Exploits: Flaws in smart contracts can lead to significant financial losses if exploited.

- 51% Attacks: In proof-of-work blockchains, a malicious entity with more than 51% of the network's computational power can manipulate transactions and double-spend coins.

Safeguarding Digital Assets: Best Practices

- Cold Storage: Storing private keys offline, or in "cold storage," can prevent them from being vulnerable to online attacks.

- Multi-Signature Wallets: Requiring multiple private keys to authorize transactions adds an extra layer of security.

- Hardware Wallets: Physical devices that store private keys securely offer a robust option for protecting digital assets.

- Security Audits: Regular security audits of smart contracts and blockchain infrastructure help identify vulnerabilities before they are exploited.

- Education: Raising awareness about common security risks and best practices among users is crucial to prevent falling victim to scams and attacks.

Regulatory Measures for Security

Regulatory bodies are increasingly focusing on security in the blockchain space:

- Licensing and Compliance: Some jurisdictions require cryptocurrency businesses to obtain licenses, demonstrating compliance with security and anti-money laundering (AML) measures.

- Consumer Protection: Regulatory frameworks often include provisions to protect consumers from fraudulent schemes and scams.

- Cybersecurity Standards: Governments and organizations are working to establish cybersecurity standards specific to blockchain technology and digital asset management.

The Ongoing Arms Race: Enhancing Security Measures

Security is an ongoing arms race between malicious actors and the defenders of the blockchain ecosystem. Key efforts include:

- Advanced Encryption Techniques: Implementing state-of-the-art encryption methods to protect private keys and user data.

- Decentralization: Distributed networks are more resilient to attacks, as no single point of failure exists.

- Immutable Records: Blockchain's immutability can be leveraged to detect tampering attempts and maintain a transparent record of activities.

- White Hat Hacking: Ethical hackers identify vulnerabilities and report them to developers, contributing to stronger security measures.

- Incident Response Plans: Developing plans to respond effectively to security breaches and minimize damage.

Building Trust in the Ecosystem

Enhancing security measures is paramount to building trust within the blockchain ecosystem:

- User Confidence: Ensuring that users have confidence in the security of their digital assets is crucial for mainstream adoption.

- Institutional Investment: Institutional investors require robust security measures to mitigate risks before entering the blockchain space.

- Regulatory Acceptance: Demonstrating a commitment to security can facilitate regulatory acceptance of blockchain projects and technologies.

Conclusion

Security is an ever-present challenge in the blockchain ecosystem, requiring constant vigilance and proactive measures to protect digital assets, users, and the overall integrity of the technology. As the blockchain landscape continues to evolve, the development of innovative security solutions, regulatory frameworks, and collaborative efforts between stakeholders will play a pivotal role in addressing security concerns and advancing the responsible and secure use of blockchain technology.

Environmental Impact: Energy Consumption and Sustainability

As the adoption of cryptocurrencies and blockchain technology has grown, concerns about their environmental impact, particularly energy consumption, have come to the forefront. The process of validating transactions and securing blockchain networks, often referred to as mining, relies on energy-intensive processes that raise questions about the sustainability of the technology. This section explores the complex relationship between blockchain technology, energy consumption, and environmental sustainability, discussing the challenges, innovative solutions, and ongoing efforts to address these environmental concerns.

Energy Consumption in Blockchain Networks

Blockchain networks use various consensus mechanisms to validate transactions and secure the network. In proof-of-work (PoW) blockchains, miners compete to solve complex mathematical puzzles, requiring significant computational power and energy consumption. The energy-intensive nature of PoW has led to concerns about its environmental impact.

The Environmental Debate

- Carbon Footprint: Critics argue that the energy consumption of blockchain networks contributes to carbon emissions and exacerbates climate change.

- Resource Usage: The high demand for computational power can lead to increased resource usage, including electricity and hardware components.

- Electronic Waste: The rapid pace of hardware obsolescence in mining operations can contribute to electronic waste.

Challenges and Considerations

The environmental impact of blockchain technology raises several challenges:

- Scalability: As blockchain networks grow, energy consumption could rise exponentially, intensifying environmental concerns.

- Renewable Energy Integration: Exploring ways to power blockchain networks using renewable energy sources is a key consideration.

- Carbon Offsetting: Some blockchain projects are exploring carbon offsetting strategies to mitigate their carbon footprint.

Innovative Solutions

Efforts are underway to reduce the environmental impact of blockchain technology:

- Proof-of-Stake (PoS): PoS consensus mechanisms, where validators are chosen based on the number of coins they hold, offer a more energy-efficient alternative to PoW.

- Hybrid Models: Some blockchain projects are exploring hybrid consensus models that combine PoW with PoS, aiming to strike a balance between security and energy efficiency.

- Energy-Efficient Hardware: Developing energy-efficient hardware specifically designed for blockchain operations can help reduce energy consumption.

- Decentralized Energy Grids: Integrating blockchain technology with decentralized energy grids could promote the use of renewable energy sources for mining operations.

Case Studies: The Carbon Footprint of Cryptocurrencies

- Bitcoin: Bitcoin's energy consumption has led to concerns about its carbon footprint, with some regions considering bans or restrictions on mining activities.

- Ethereum: Ethereum's planned transition from PoW to PoS through Ethereum 2.0 is expected to significantly reduce its energy consumption.

- Proof-of-Stake Networks: Cryptocurrencies like Cardano (ADA) and Algorand (ALGO) operate on PoS networks, substantially lowering their energy consumption.

Collaborative Efforts

- Green Mining Initiatives: Some mining operations are shifting toward using renewable energy sources and adopting sustainable practices.

- Carbon Reporting: Transparently reporting energy consumption and carbon emissions can provide insights into the environmental impact of blockchain networks.

- Industry Standards: Developing energy efficiency standards and guidelines specific to blockchain technology could promote responsible use.

Balancing Innovation and Sustainability

Balancing the innovative potential of blockchain technology with environmental sustainability requires:

- Long-Term Vision: Incorporating sustainable practices from the design phase of blockchain projects can lead to more environmentally responsible networks.

- Regulatory Considerations: Regulatory frameworks could incentivize energy-efficient practices and discourage excessive energy consumption.

- Public Awareness: Raising awareness among blockchain users about the environmental impact of their activities can promote more responsible behavior.

Conclusion

Addressing the environmental impact of blockchain technology is a complex challenge that requires collaboration between stakeholders, innovation in consensus mechanisms, and the integration of sustainable practices. As the blockchain ecosystem evolves, striking a balance between the benefits of the technology and its impact on the environment is crucial for ensuring the responsible and sustainable growth of the industry.

Social and Economic Implications: Disruption and Adoption

The rapid rise of cryptocurrencies and blockchain technology has not only transformed the technological landscape but has also brought about profound social and economic implications. From disrupting traditional financial systems to fostering financial inclusion and changing the dynamics of industries, this section delves into the multifaceted impact of blockchain technology on society and the global economy. We'll explore both the disruptive potential and the opportunities for adoption, discussing how blockchain technology has the potential to reshape various sectors, alter power dynamics, and empower individuals in unprecedented ways.

Disrupting Traditional Industries

Blockchain technology is disrupting a wide range of industries, challenging existing norms and business models:

Finance: Cryptocurrencies and blockchain have the potential to revolutionize traditional banking systems, enabling peer-to-peer financial transactions, reducing fees, and improving access to financial services, especially in underserved regions.

Supply Chain: Blockchain's transparent and immutable ledger can enhance supply chain transparency, traceability, and authenticity verification, mitigating fraud and ensuring ethical practices.

Healthcare: Blockchain can facilitate secure and interoperable data sharing among healthcare providers, improving patient care, data accuracy, and medical research.

Real Estate: Blockchain-based property registries can streamline the buying and selling of real estate, reducing fraud and increasing transparency in property transactions.

Disrupting Power Structures

Blockchain technology also has the potential to reshape power dynamics in various ways:

Decentralization: Decentralized networks challenge the concentration of power in centralized institutions, giving more agency to individuals and reducing the need for intermediaries.

Financial Inclusion: Blockchain enables access to financial services for the unbanked and underbanked populations, allowing them to participate in the global economy.

Data Ownership: Blockchain can empower individuals by giving them control over their own data, allowing them to monetize it and decide who has access.

Smart Contracts: Self-executing smart contracts can automate agreements and transactions, reducing the need for intermediaries and increasing efficiency.

Opportunities for Adoption

While blockchain poses disruptive challenges, its adoption also presents significant opportunities:

Efficiency Gains: By streamlining processes, reducing intermediaries, and minimizing paperwork, blockchain can lead to efficiency gains across industries.

Reduced Fraud: Blockchain's transparency and immutability can reduce fraudulent activities, boosting consumer trust and protecting businesses.

Cross-Border Transactions: Cryptocurrencies enable faster and cheaper cross-border transactions, eliminating the need for intermediaries like correspondent banks.

Micropayments: Blockchain facilitates micropayments, opening up new revenue streams for content creators and artists.

Global Trade: Blockchain can simplify and secure global trade processes, reducing paperwork, delays, and errors.

Challenges and Considerations

Despite the opportunities, adopting blockchain technology is not without challenges:

Regulatory Uncertainty: Differing regulatory approaches globally can hinder the widespread adoption of blockchain solutions.

Technical Hurdles: Integrating legacy systems with blockchain technology and ensuring scalability can be technically complex.

User Education: Widespread adoption requires educating users about the benefits, risks, and proper usage of blockchain solutions.

Interoperability: Ensuring that different blockchain networks can communicate and work together seamlessly is a challenge.

Inclusivity: Ensuring that the benefits of blockchain technology reach marginalized communities and underserved regions is essential for fostering equality.

Conclusion

The social and economic implications of blockchain technology are vast and multifaceted. As the technology continues to evolve and mature, its transformative potential becomes more evident. While the disruption of traditional systems and industries may bring challenges, it also offers opportunities for innovation, efficiency, and empowerment. Striking a balance between harnessing the disruptive power of blockchain technology and addressing the challenges it presents will be crucial for realizing its full potential and creating a more inclusive, transparent, and efficient global economy.

Chapter 7: The Decentralized Future
Decentralized Governance: DAOs and Community Consensus

The concept of decentralized governance is at the heart of blockchain technology's promise to reshape power dynamics and decision-making processes. Decentralized Autonomous Organizations (DAOs) and community consensus mechanisms are innovative approaches that aim to replace traditional hierarchical structures with participatory and inclusive governance models. In this section, we explore the evolution of decentralized governance, the principles behind DAOs, the challenges and opportunities they present, and the potential for these models to shape the future of organizations and communities.

Evolution of Governance: From Centralization to Decentralization

Traditional governance models are often centralized, relying on hierarchical structures and top-down decision-making. With the emergence of blockchain technology, the potential for decentralized governance became apparent, allowing individuals to participate in decision-making processes directly.

Principles of Decentralized Governance

Decentralized governance models are built on key principles:

- Transparency: All actions and decisions are recorded on a public ledger, ensuring transparency and accountability.

- Inclusivity: Anyone can participate in decision-making, irrespective of geographical location or socio-economic status.

- Immutable Rules: Decisions are executed based on predefined smart contracts, preventing arbitrary changes.

- Security: Blockchain's security mechanisms ensure the integrity of voting and decision-making processes.

Decentralized Autonomous Organizations (DAOs)

DAOs are organizations governed by code, allowing stakeholders to make decisions collectively through voting mechanisms encoded on a blockchain. DAOs represent a new paradigm of governance that eliminates intermediaries and enables stakeholders to manage resources and make decisions autonomously.

How DAOs Work

- Smart Contracts: DAOs use smart contracts to define rules and decision-making processes, ensuring transparency and accountability.

- Voting Mechanisms: Stakeholders participate in decisions by voting on proposals, with voting power often determined by the number of tokens held.

- Resource Allocation: DAOs allocate resources, such as funding for projects, based on the consensus of the stakeholders.

Challenges and Opportunities

- Complex Decision-Making: Ensuring that complex decisions are made efficiently and fairly within DAOs can be challenging.

- Security and Vulnerabilities: Smart contracts are vulnerable to bugs and vulnerabilities that could be exploited, leading to unintended consequences.

- Governance Coordination: Coordinating the diverse opinions and interests of stakeholders within a DAO can be difficult.

- Incentive Alignment: Ensuring that participants' incentives are aligned with the organization's goals is crucial for DAO success.

Real-World Examples of DAOs

- MakerDAO: A decentralized autonomous organization that manages the stablecoin DAI and maintains its value through smart contracts.

- Aragon: A platform for creating and managing DAOs, empowering communities to make collective decisions.

- MolochDAO: A funding DAO focused on supporting Ethereum development projects through community-driven decisions.

Community Consensus Mechanisms

Decentralized governance extends beyond DAOs to community consensus mechanisms that allow for collective decision-making in decentralized networks.

- Proof of Stake: Validators in PoS blockchains propose and validate transactions while participating in governance decisions.

- Decentralized Voting: Token holders participate in voting to decide on network upgrades, changes, and resource allocations.

The Future of Decentralized Governance

Decentralized governance models hold the potential to reshape organizational structures and democratize decision-making:

- Disintermediation: By removing intermediaries, decentralized governance reduces power concentration and fosters inclusion.

- Collaborative Innovation: DAOs can accelerate innovation by enabling community-driven development and funding.

- Global Collaboration: Decentralized governance facilitates collaboration on a global scale, transcending geographical boundaries.

- Challenges and Maturity: Overcoming challenges in DAO governance, such as avoiding plutocracy, remains a critical task for their widespread adoption.

Governance Beyond Blockchain

The principles of decentralized governance extend beyond the realm of blockchain technology, influencing broader discussions about the future of democracy, corporate governance, and collaborative decision-making.

Conclusion

Decentralized governance models represent a revolutionary shift in how organizations and communities make decisions. By leveraging blockchain technology's transparency, immutability, and inclusivity, DAOs and community consensus mechanisms have the potential to redefine power structures, enhance collaboration, and democratize decision-making processes. The evolution and maturation of these models will play a pivotal role in shaping the decentralized future, where participants have a direct say in the development of projects, communities, and even broader societal systems.

Web3.0: The Decentralized Internet

The evolution of the internet has undergone several transformative phases, each bringing new capabilities and opportunities. Web3.0, often referred to as the decentralized internet, represents the next stage of this evolution by integrating blockchain technology and decentralized principles into the fabric of the internet. In this section, we explore the concept of Web3.0, its foundational principles, the potential it holds for reshaping online interactions and industries, and the challenges and opportunities on the path to realizing a truly decentralized online world.

Understanding Web3.0: The Evolution of the Internet

- Web1.0: The static and informational era of the early internet, where websites provided static content for users to consume.

- Web2.0: The social and interactive web, characterized by user-generated content, social media platforms, and dynamic applications.

- Web3.0: The decentralized web, integrating blockchain technology to empower users with ownership of data, privacy control, and peer-to-peer interactions.

Foundational Principles of Web3.0

Web3.0 is built on several core principles that distinguish it from its predecessors:

- Decentralization: Distributed networks and blockchain technology replace central authorities, reducing the power of tech giants and fostering a more democratic internet.

- User Empowerment: Users have greater control over their data, privacy settings, and online identity, reducing the dependency on platform providers.

- Interoperability: Different blockchain networks and applications can communicate seamlessly, enabling a unified and cohesive online experience.

- Data Ownership: Users own and control their data, and they can monetize it or share it with permission in exchange for value.

Impact on Online Interactions and Industries

- Data Privacy: Web3.0 enhances user privacy, enabling users to share data on their terms and reducing the risks of large-scale data breaches.

- Content Ownership: Creators have direct ownership and control over their content, reducing the reliance on platforms for distribution and monetization.

- Digital Identity: Users have self-sovereign identities that are not tied to any centralized authority, enhancing security and privacy.

- E-Commerce and Micropayments: Direct peer-to-peer transactions are facilitated by cryptocurrencies, enabling efficient micropayments and reducing intermediaries in e-commerce.

Challenges on the Path to Web3.0

- Usability: Web3.0 technologies can be complex and daunting for mainstream users, hindering adoption.

- Scalability: Integrating blockchain into the internet infrastructure poses scalability challenges, particularly in terms of transaction speeds and network capacity.

- Regulatory Uncertainty: The regulatory environment for Web3.0 is evolving, posing challenges for developers and users.

- Education and Awareness: Educating users about the benefits, risks, and mechanics of Web3.0 is crucial for its widespread adoption.

Realizing the Vision of Web3.0

Several projects and initiatives are working to realize the vision of Web3.0:

- IPFS (InterPlanetary File System): A protocol designed to create a peer-to-peer method of storing and sharing hypermedia in a distributed file system.

- Polkadot: A multi-chain blockchain platform that enables different blockchain networks to interoperate and share information.

- Solid: An initiative by Tim Berners-Lee, the inventor of the World Wide Web, aiming to give users control over their personal data and online interactions.

Web3.0 in Practice: Use Cases

- Decentralized Social Media: Platforms like Mastodon and Steemit are experimenting with decentralized social media, enabling users to own and control their content.

- Decentralized Finance (DeFi): DeFi applications operate on decentralized networks, enabling peer-to-peer financial interactions without intermediaries.

- Decentralized Identity: Sovrin and uPort are working on self-sovereign identity solutions that give users control over their digital identities.

The Future of Web3.0: Beyond Technology

Web3.0's impact goes beyond technology:

- Societal Shifts: Web3.0 challenges the dominance of tech giants, potentially reshaping power dynamics and reducing centralization.

- Economic Transformation: New business models based on peer-to-peer interactions and decentralized applications may emerge.

- Digital Inclusion: Web3.0 could bridge the digital divide by providing access to online resources and services in underserved regions.

Conclusion

Web3.0 represents a paradigm shift in the way we interact with the internet, emphasizing user empowerment, data ownership, and decentralization. As the technology and concepts mature, the decentralized internet holds the promise of fostering a more democratic, privacy-focused, and user-centric online world. However, realizing this vision requires overcoming technical challenges, regulatory hurdles, and the need for widespread education and awareness. Web3.0 has the potential to reshape online interactions, industries, and power dynamics, paving the way for a truly decentralized and inclusive digital future.

The Potential of Cryptocurrencies: Financial Inclusion and Empowerment

Cryptocurrencies have emerged as a powerful tool with the potential to transform financial systems, providing avenues for financial inclusion and empowerment that were previously unimaginable. In this section, we explore how cryptocurrencies can address the challenges of traditional financial systems, the impact on underserved populations, and the opportunities for reshaping global economies through greater financial accessibility and autonomy.

Challenges of Traditional Financial Systems

- Lack of Access: A significant portion of the global population lacks access to traditional financial services, such as banking and credit.

- High Fees: Traditional financial systems often come with high transaction fees and hidden charges, especially for cross-border transactions.

- Limited Transparency: Centralized financial systems can lack transparency, making it difficult to verify transactions and ensure accountability.

The Promise of Financial Inclusion

Cryptocurrencies have the potential to address these challenges and promote financial inclusion:

- Global Accessibility: Anyone with an internet connection can access and use cryptocurrencies, bridging the gap for those without traditional banking services.

- Low Transaction Fees: Cryptocurrency transactions can be conducted with minimal fees, particularly in comparison to cross-border transfers.

- Transparency and Security: Transactions are recorded on a public ledger, enhancing transparency and security.

Cryptocurrencies for Underserved Populations

- Unbanked and Underbanked: Cryptocurrencies provide a way for individuals without access to traditional banking services to participate in the global economy.

- Remittances: Cryptocurrencies enable cost-effective cross-border remittances, allowing individuals to send funds to their families without hefty fees.

- Micropayments: Cryptocurrencies make micropayments viable, creating new economic opportunities for content creators and artists.

Empowering Individuals through Financial Autonomy

- Self-Custody: Users have direct control over their funds, eliminating the need for intermediaries like banks.

- Financial Sovereignty: Cryptocurrencies enable individuals to manage their wealth independently of centralized institutions.

- Monetary Inclusion: In regions with unstable or hyperinflated currencies, cryptocurrencies can provide stability and a store of value.

Challenges and Considerations

While cryptocurrencies offer significant potential for financial inclusion and empowerment, challenges persist:

- Volatility: Cryptocurrency prices can be highly volatile, posing risks for those who rely on them for stability.

- Technical Barriers: Cryptocurrency adoption requires digital literacy and access to technology, which can be barriers for some populations.

- Regulatory Uncertainty: Varying regulatory approaches globally can impact the legality and acceptance of cryptocurrencies.

- Security Concerns: Ensuring the security of private keys and wallets is crucial to prevent loss of funds.

Use Cases and Success Stories

- Stablecoins: Cryptocurrencies pegged to stable assets like fiat currencies can provide stability and facilitate everyday transactions.

- Mobile Money in Developing Countries: Cryptocurrencies are being used to create mobile money systems, providing financial services to the unbanked.

- Cross-Border Transactions: Cryptocurrencies like Bitcoin have been used to facilitate cross-border trade and transactions in regions with limited access to traditional banking.

Reshaping Global Economies

- Financial Empowerment: Cryptocurrencies can shift power from financial intermediaries to individuals, enabling more direct control over one's financial future.

- Remittances and Cross-Border Trade: Cryptocurrencies can streamline cross-border trade and remittance processes, promoting economic growth.

- Economic Participation: Cryptocurrencies enable individuals to participate in the global economy, fostering entrepreneurship and innovation.

Collaborative Initiatives for Inclusion

- Education and Awareness: Educating underserved populations about cryptocurrencies' benefits and risks is crucial for their effective use.

- Partnerships: Collaborations between governments, nonprofits, and the private sector can facilitate the adoption of cryptocurrencies for financial inclusion.

Conclusion

Cryptocurrencies have the potential to reshape the financial landscape by promoting financial inclusion, autonomy, and empowerment. By providing a means for underserved populations to access financial services, conduct cross-border transactions, and manage their wealth independently, cryptocurrencies can contribute to a more equitable and accessible global economy. While challenges remain, including volatility, technical barriers, and regulatory uncertainties, collaborative efforts and innovative use cases are paving the way for cryptocurrencies to play a significant role in fostering financial inclusion and empowering individuals worldwide.

Exploring New Frontiers: Quantum Resistance and Post-Blockchain Technologies

The evolution of decentralized technology does not end with the current state of blockchain. Emerging challenges, such as the potential threat from quantum computers to existing cryptographic methods, and the need for scalability and efficiency improvements, have spurred the exploration of new frontiers. In this section, we delve into the concept of quantum resistance, the limitations of current blockchain technology, and the exciting possibilities offered by post-blockchain technologies.

Quantum Computing and Cryptography

- Quantum Threat: Quantum computers, when realized at scale, have the potential to break existing cryptographic methods used to secure blockchain networks.

- Current Cryptography: Most blockchain systems rely on cryptographic methods that could be vulnerable to attacks by powerful quantum computers.

Quantum Resistance: The Next Frontier

- Quantum-Resistant Cryptography: Research is ongoing to develop cryptographic methods that are resistant to quantum attacks, ensuring the security of blockchain networks.

- Lattice-Based Cryptography: Lattice-based cryptography is one approach being explored to achieve quantum resistance.

- Transition Challenges: Transitioning existing blockchain networks to quantum-resistant cryptography poses challenges but is essential for long-term security.

Limitations of Current Blockchain Technology

- Scalability: Current blockchain networks face challenges in handling a large number of transactions at high speeds.

- Energy Efficiency: Proof-of-work blockchains consume significant energy, leading to concerns about sustainability.

- Interoperability: Blockchains often operate in isolation, limiting interoperability between different networks.

Post-Blockchain Technologies

- Directed Acyclic Graphs (DAGs): DAGs represent a different data structure than traditional blockchains and offer potential for scalability and efficiency improvements.

- Hashgraph: Hashgraph is a consensus mechanism that promises high throughput, low latency, and fairness.

- Tangle: Tangle is a data structure used in IOTA, designed for the Internet of Things, that aims to overcome scalability and fee challenges.

- Holochain: Holochain is a framework for creating decentralized applications with agent-centric data models, enabling greater scalability.

Beyond Cryptocurrency: Use Cases for Post-Blockchain Technologies

- Decentralized Applications (dApps): Post-blockchain technologies enable dApps with faster transaction speeds and improved user experiences.

- Supply Chain Management: Efficiently tracking and verifying supply chains can benefit from the scalability and transparency offered by post-blockchain technologies.

- IoT and Data Integrity: The Internet of Things requires scalable and efficient solutions for managing large volumes of data with integrity.

Challenges and Considerations

- Adoption Challenges: Transitioning from established blockchain networks to new technologies requires coordination and incentivizing migration.

- Security Concerns: New technologies must be thoroughly tested to ensure security and avoid vulnerabilities.

- Economic Models: Creating sustainable economic models for new technologies, including tokenomics and incentives, is crucial for their success.

The Road Ahead: Balancing Innovation and Stability

- Balancing Act: Striking a balance between adopting innovative technologies and maintaining the stability and security of existing systems is crucial.

- Collaborative Research: Collaborations between academia, industry, and the wider community are essential for advancing post-blockchain technologies.

- Regulatory Adaptation: Regulatory frameworks may need to adapt to accommodate new technological paradigms while ensuring security and accountability.

Conclusion

As blockchain technology continues to evolve, the exploration of new frontiers becomes imperative to address emerging challenges and seize opportunities for scalability, efficiency, and security. Quantum resistance and post-blockchain technologies represent exciting possibilities for creating more secure and adaptable decentralized systems. By harnessing quantum-resistant cryptography and embracing innovative data structures and consensus mechanisms, the decentralized future can be shaped to address current limitations and pave the way for a more inclusive, efficient, and secure digital landscape.

Conclusion

The Cypherpunk Ideals in a Cryptocurrency World

The journey through the world of cryptocurrencies and decentralized technologies has been a remarkable exploration of the convergence of technological innovation, philosophical ideals, and socio-economic transformation. As we conclude our exploration of the cypherpunk legacy and the profound impact of decentralized systems, it is crucial to reflect on how the ideals that motivated early cypherpunks continue to resonate in the context of the cryptocurrency world. This concluding chapter revisits the core principles of the cypherpunk movement, assesses their manifestation in cryptocurrencies, and contemplates the ongoing and future implications of these ideals in shaping the decentralized future.

The Cypherpunk Ethos Revisited

- Privacy as a Right: Privacy was a foundational principle for cypherpunks, and cryptocurrencies have embraced this ideal through pseudonymous transactions, advanced cryptography, and self-sovereign identities.

- Decentralization and Autonomy: The pursuit of decentralization and individual autonomy in cyberspace remains a driving force behind cryptocurrencies, reshaping power dynamics and challenging centralized control.

- Encryption and Security: Cryptocurrencies have advanced cryptographic techniques to secure transactions, data, and communication, aligning with the cypherpunk commitment to robust encryption.

Cryptocurrencies as Manifestations of Cypherpunk Ideals

- Privacy Coins: Privacy-focused cryptocurrencies like Monero and Zcash have built on the cypherpunk emphasis on private and pseudonymous transactions.

- Decentralized Networks: The architecture of decentralized blockchain networks embodies the vision of autonomous, censorship-resistant communication that cypherpunks championed.

- Self-Sovereign Identity: The concept of self-sovereign identity, a cornerstone of cypherpunk philosophy, is being realized through blockchain-based identity solutions.

Balancing Ideals with Reality

- Regulatory Landscape: Cryptocurrencies operate in a complex regulatory environment, prompting discussions about balancing privacy with legal compliance.

- Accessibility and Inclusion: The challenge of ensuring widespread accessibility to cryptocurrencies while maintaining privacy and security echoes the cypherpunk aim for inclusion.

- Environmental Concerns: The energy consumption of some blockchain networks raises questions about the environmental sustainability of decentralized technologies.

The Ongoing Evolution of Decentralized Ideals

- Technological Innovation: The rapid evolution of blockchain technology continues to push the boundaries of what's possible in terms of privacy, security, and scalability.

- Social and Economic Implications: The increasing impact of cryptocurrencies on finance, economics, and society underscores the need to navigate the delicate balance between disruption and stability.

Cryptocurrencies as Agents of Change

- Financial Inclusion: Cryptocurrencies have the potential to break down barriers to financial access, aligning with cypherpunk ideals of empowering individuals.

- Reshaping Power Structures: The shift towards decentralized systems challenges established power structures and places more control in the hands of individuals.

The Road Ahead: Embracing the Decentralized Future

- Education and Awareness: Educating users about the benefits, risks, and technical aspects of cryptocurrencies is crucial for responsible adoption.

- Regulatory Frameworks: Striking the right balance between innovation and regulation will shape how cryptocurrencies integrate into existing legal systems.

- Global Collaboration: The decentralized future requires collaboration between governments, tech communities, and individuals to address challenges and maximize benefits.

The Unfinished Story of Decentralization

As we conclude this exploration, it's important to recognize that the story of decentralization is far from finished. The cypherpunk ideals that sparked the movement continue to inspire and evolve in the cryptocurrency world. The pursuit of privacy, autonomy, and empowerment, combined with technological innovation, is shaping a future where individuals have greater control over their digital lives and the systems that govern them. While challenges persist and the path forward may be complex, the decentralized future holds the potential to reshape not only technology but also the very fabric of society, offering new opportunities for collaboration, empowerment, and progress.

Balancing Privacy, Security, and Regulation

The journey through the intricate landscape of cryptocurrencies and decentralized technologies has brought to light the delicate interplay between privacy, security, and regulatory considerations. As we draw our exploration to a close, it is crucial to reflect on the paramount importance of achieving a harmonious equilibrium between these three fundamental pillars. This concluding chapter delves into the complexities of balancing privacy, security, and regulation in the context of decentralized systems, emphasizing the challenges, opportunities, and potential paths forward.

The Inseparable Trio: Privacy, Security, and Regulation

- Privacy as a Fundamental Right: Privacy is a foundational value enshrined in both human rights and cypherpunk ethos, underpinning the development of pseudonymous transactions and cryptographic techniques.

- Security at the Core: The security of blockchain networks is paramount, with cryptographic algorithms and consensus mechanisms designed to safeguard against attacks.

- Regulation as a Balancing Act: Regulatory frameworks are essential to prevent misuse and illicit activities, but they must be carefully designed to avoid stifling innovation.

Navigating the Privacy Landscape

- Pseudonymity and Anonymity: Cryptocurrencies offer varying degrees of privacy, ranging from fully anonymous transactions to pseudonymous identities.

- Balancing Transparency: Striking a balance between transparency and privacy is a challenge, as transparent transactions are essential for accountability and traceability.

- Enhancing Privacy Technologies: Zero-knowledge proofs, ring signatures, and other cryptographic techniques are continually evolving to enhance privacy without compromising security.

Security in a Decentralized World

- Cryptography and Integrity: Cryptographic algorithms ensure the integrity of data and transactions, preventing unauthorized access and tampering.

- Consensus Mechanisms: Proof-of-work and proof-of-stake mechanisms secure blockchain networks and maintain the trustless nature of decentralized systems.

- Smart Contract Auditing: Ensuring the security of smart contracts is vital to prevent vulnerabilities that could lead to financial losses or network disruptions.

Regulation and the Boundaries of Innovation

- Avoiding Overregulation: Striking the right balance between regulation and innovation is crucial to prevent stifling the potential of decentralized technologies.

- Global Collaboration: The decentralized nature of cryptocurrencies presents challenges in crafting uniform regulatory approaches across borders.

- Regulating the Unregulated: Regulators are grappling with how to fit cryptocurrencies into existing regulatory frameworks designed for traditional financial instruments.

Protecting User Rights and Interests

- Consumer Protection: Regulatory efforts must focus on protecting consumers from fraud, scams, and risks associated with the volatility of cryptocurrencies.

- Data Privacy: Balancing data privacy regulations with the transparent nature of blockchain presents challenges in safeguarding sensitive information.

The Potential Pathways Forward

- Education and Awareness: An informed public is essential for responsible engagement with cryptocurrencies and decentralized systems.

- Industry Standards: Establishing industry-wide security and privacy standards can provide a framework for innovation while ensuring user safety.

- Adaptive Regulation: Regulatory frameworks need to be agile and adaptive to technological advancements while addressing concerns of financial stability and consumer protection.

A Collaborative Approach

- Tech and Policy Collaboration: Bridging the gap between technological development and regulatory policy is essential for comprehensive and effective oversight.

- Engaging Stakeholders: Collaborative efforts involving governments, academia, industry, and civil society can lead to holistic solutions that address privacy, security, and regulatory concerns.

The Road Ahead: A Balanced Decentralized Future

As we conclude this exploration, the path forward lies in embracing a future where privacy, security, and regulation coexist in harmony. Cryptocurrencies and decentralized technologies are not only reshaping the digital landscape but also challenging conventional paradigms of governance and control. By fostering an environment that values innovation, consumer protection, and user autonomy, we can navigate the complexities of decentralization with a holistic perspective, ultimately creating a decentralized future that upholds the principles of privacy, security, and responsible regulation. The journey is ongoing, and it is up to the collective efforts of society to steer this transformative evolution towards a balanced and inclusive decentralized future.

Embracing the Decentralized Future

The expedition into the realm of cryptocurrencies and decentralized technologies has illuminated a profound shift in the way we perceive and interact with systems of value, trust, and governance. As we conclude our exploration, it is imperative to delve into the essence of embracing the decentralized future – a future that holds promises of empowerment, inclusivity, and transformative potential. This concluding chapter delves into the core principles that underpin the decentralized movement, the societal and economic ramifications of this evolution, and the imperative for collective action in navigating the uncharted waters of decentralization.

The Core Principles of the Decentralized Movement

- Empowerment Through Autonomy: Decentralization puts individuals in control of their digital lives, fostering autonomy and challenging traditional power dynamics.

- Inclusivity and Accessibility: The decentralized landscape is opening doors to individuals who were once excluded from financial and technological systems.

- Transparency and Trustlessness: Trust is established through transparent, verifiable, and immutable transactions, diminishing the need for intermediaries.

Economic and Societal Transformations

- Disrupting Traditional Finance: Cryptocurrencies have the potential to reshape traditional financial structures, enabling new ways of transacting, saving, and investing.

- Fostering Innovation: Decentralized systems encourage innovation by providing a playground for experimentation and unearthing new use cases.

- Digital Sovereignty: Individuals gaining control over their digital identity and assets challenge the centralization of data by tech giants.

Challenges and Opportunities of the Decentralized Future

- Scalability and Efficiency: Overcoming the scalability challenge is key to realizing the mass adoption of decentralized systems.

- Regulatory Navigation: Striking a balance between regulation and innovation is critical to nurturing a thriving decentralized ecosystem.

- Environmental Responsibility: Addressing the energy consumption of certain consensus mechanisms is essential for the sustainability of the decentralized future.

Decentralization in Real-World Applications

- Decentralized Finance (DeFi): DeFi is reshaping traditional financial services, offering accessibility, transparency, and peer-to-peer transactions.

- Digital Identity: Self-sovereign identity solutions empower individuals to control their digital personas, enhancing privacy and security.

- Supply Chain Management: The transparency offered by blockchain technology is revolutionizing supply chain tracking, ensuring authenticity and ethical practices.

The Imperative for Collective Action

- Global Collaboration: Decentralization transcends borders, necessitating collaboration between governments, industry, academia, and civil society.

- Education and Awareness: Educating the public about the potential and risks of decentralization is paramount for responsible engagement.

- Ethical Considerations: Ethical frameworks must be developed to guide the use of decentralized technologies, preventing potential misuse.

Paving the Path Forward

- Technology and Regulation Synergy: Effective regulation should be technology-informed, striking a balance between innovation and security.

- Empowering Individuals: Nurturing a decentralized future involves empowering individuals to take ownership of their digital experiences.

- Striving for Sustainability: The decentralized future must be built on sustainable and environmentally responsible practices.

The Unwritten Chapters of Decentralization

As we conclude this expedition, it is essential to recognize that the journey into decentralization is far from over. The vision of a decentralized future is dynamic and constantly evolving, adapting to technological advancements, societal needs, and regulatory frameworks. The ideals of empowerment, inclusivity, and transparency that guide this movement offer a glimpse into a world where individuals have greater control over their digital lives and the structures that govern them. The chapters yet unwritten hold the promise of a future where decentralized technologies continue to bridge divides, foster innovation, and shape a society that values autonomy and empowerment. It is a future that we collectively build, one where the principles of decentralization remain at the forefront, lighting the path towards a more equitable, open, and decentralized world.

THE END

Wordbook

Welcome to the glossary section of this book. Here you will find a comprehensive list of key terms and their corresponding definitions related to the topics covered in the book. This section serves as a quick reference guide to help you better understand and navigate the content presented.

Key terms

1. Cryptocurrency: A digital or virtual form of money that uses cryptography for secure transactions, control of new units creation, and verification of asset transfers on a decentralized network, typically based on blockchain technology.

2. Decentralization: The distribution of control, authority, and decision-making across a network of participants rather than being centralized in a single entity or authority.

3. Cypherpunk: A person who advocates for privacy-enhancing technologies, cryptography, and digital autonomy to protect individual freedoms and privacy rights in the digital age.

4. Blockchain: A distributed and immutable digital ledger that records transactions across multiple computers in a way that ensures security, transparency, and consensus without the need for a central authority.

5. Pseudonymous Transactions: Transactions that use pseudonyms or aliases instead of real names, enhancing privacy by concealing the identity of transaction participants.

6. Proof-of-Work (PoW): A consensus mechanism used in blockchain networks where participants (miners) solve complex mathematical problems to validate transactions and create new blocks, requiring significant computational effort.

7. Proof-of-Stake (PoS): A consensus mechanism that validates transactions and creates new blocks based on the amount of cryptocurrency held and "staked" by participants, reducing the energy consumption compared to PoW.

8. Smart Contracts: Self-executing contracts with predefined rules and conditions that are automatically enforced on the blockchain when certain conditions are met.

9. Decentralized Finance (DeFi): Financial applications built on blockchain networks that provide decentralized alternatives to traditional financial services, including lending, borrowing, trading, and yield farming.

10. Privacy Coin: A type of cryptocurrency designed to enhance user privacy by implementing advanced cryptographic techniques to obfuscate transaction details and sender/receiver information.

11. Zero-Knowledge Proof: A cryptographic method that allows one party to prove to another that they know a specific piece of information without revealing the actual information itself.

12. Quantum Resistance: The quality of a cryptographic algorithm that remains secure even against attacks from quantum computers, which have the potential to break traditional cryptographic methods.

13. Hashgraph: A consensus mechanism that uses a directed acyclic graph (DAG) structure to achieve high throughput and low latency in transaction processing.

14. Tangle: A DAG-based architecture used in IOTA's blockchain alternative that aims to provide a scalable and feeless platform for the Internet of Things (IoT).

15. Self-Sovereign Identity: An individual's ownership and control over their personal identity data, allowing them to share information as needed while maintaining privacy and security.

16. Stablecoin: A type of cryptocurrency designed to maintain a stable value by pegging it to a reserve of assets, such as a fiat currency or commodity.

17. Interoperability: The ability of different blockchain networks or protocols to communicate and work together

seamlessly, allowing the transfer of assets and data across various platforms.

18. Regulatory Frameworks: Laws, regulations, and guidelines established by governments and regulatory bodies to govern the use, trading, and taxation of cryptocurrencies and related technologies.

19. Tokenomics: The economic model and structure of a cryptocurrency or token, including its distribution, utility, and incentive mechanisms.

20. Decentralized Autonomous Organization (DAO): An organization governed by a set of pre-defined rules and smart contracts, operated by its members through consensus-based decision-making.

Supplementary Materials

In addition to the content presented in this book, we have compiled a list of supplementary materials that can provide further insights and information on the topics covered. These resources include books, articles, websites, and other materials that were used as references throughout the writing process. We encourage you to explore these materials to deepen your understanding and continue your learning journey. Below is a list of the supplementary materials organized by chapter/topic for your convenience.

Introduction:

Nakamoto, S. (2008). Bitcoin: A Peer-to-Peer Electronic Cash System. https://bitcoin.org/bitcoin.pdf

Levy, S. (2011). Crypto: How the Code Rebels Beat the Government—Saving Privacy in the Digital Age. Penguin.

Popper, N. (2016). Digital Gold: Bitcoin and the Inside Story of the Misfits and Millionaires Trying to Reinvent Money. HarperCollins.

Chapter 1: Bitcoin: The First Cryptocurrency

Antonopoulos, A. M. (2014). Mastering Bitcoin: Unlocking Digital Cryptocurrencies. O'Reilly Media.

Narayanan, A., Bonneau, J., Felten, E., Miller, A., & Goldfeder, S. (2016). Bitcoin and Cryptocurrency

Technologies: A Comprehensive Introduction. Princeton University Press.

Chapter 2: Altcoins and the Expansion of Cryptocurrency

Casey, M. J., & Vigna, P. (2018). The Truth Machine: The Blockchain and the Future of Everything. St. Martin's Press.

Buterin, V. (2013). Ethereum White Paper: A Next-Generation Smart Contract and Decentralized Application Platform. https://ethereum.org/whitepaper/

Chapter 3: Privacy Coins and Anonymity

Miers, I., Garman, C., Green, M., & Rubin, A. D. (2013). Zerocoin: Anonymous Distributed E-Cash from Bitcoin. IEEE Security & Privacy, 11(4), 52-59.

Sarang, N., Miers, I., Green, M., & Drouin, R. (2017). The Mechanics of the MimbleWimble Protocol. https://download.wpsoftware.net/bitcoin/wizardry/mimblewimble.pdf

Chapter 4: Blockchain Beyond Currency

Swan, M. (2015). Blockchain: Blueprint for a New Economy. O'Reilly Media.

Tapscott, D., & Tapscott, A. (2016). Blockchain Revolution: How the Technology Behind Bitcoin is Changing Money, Business, and the World. Penguin.

Chapter 5: Scalability and Interoperability

Poon, J., & Dryja, T. (2016). The Bitcoin Lightning Network: Scalable Off-Chain Instant Payments.

https://lightning.network/lightning-network-paper.pdf

Kosba, A., Miller, A., Shi, E., Wen, Z., & Papamanthou, C. (2016). Hawk: The Blockchain Model of Cryptography and Privacy-Preserving Smart Contracts. In Proceedings of IEEE Symposium on Security and Privacy.

Chapter 6: Regulation and Challenges

Narula, N., & Miller, A. (2017). A Survey of Cryptographic Approaches to Securing Digital Payments. IEEE Security & Privacy, 15(4), 24-39.

Peck, M. (2016). The Mysterious Disappearance of Satoshi Nakamoto, Founder of Bitcoin.

https://spectrum.ieee.org/tech-history/cyberspace/the-mysterious-disappearance-of-satoshi-nakamoto-founder-of-bitcoin

Chapter 7: The Decentralized Future

Tapscott, D., & Tapscott, A. (2020). The Supply Chain Has No Clothes. Harvard Business Review.

https://hbr.org/2020/04/the-supply-chain-has-no-clothes

Dhillon, G., & Metcalf, A. (2019). Decentralised Finance: On Blockchain- and Smart Contract-Based Financial Markets. The Journal of Risk Finance, 20(1), 13-17.

Conclusion:

Golumbia, D. (2016). The Politics of Bitcoin: Software as Right-Wing Extremism. University of Minnesota Press.

Lee, T. B. (2015). The Great Chain of Being Sure about Things. The New Yorker. https://www.newyorker.com/magazine/2015/10/12/the-cobweb

www.ingramcontent.com/pod-product-compliance
Lightning Source LLC
LaVergne TN
LVHW012107070526
838202LV00056B/5653